Cultivating Exceptional Classrooms

Unmasking Missing Links
to Achieve Quality Education

JULIE COLES

Cultivating Exceptional Classrooms:
Unmasking Missing Links to Achieve Quality Education
by Julie Coles

Copyright © 2023 Julie Coles

All rights reserved. No portion of this book may be shared without express written permission of the author. Nor may any part of this publication be reproduced, stored in a retrieval system, or transmitted in any form or by any means, electronic, mechanical, photocopying, recording, scanning, or otherwise, without the prior written permission of the author.

Developmental Editors:	Ebonye Gussine Wilkins, Inclusive Media Solutions LLC
	Brittany Dowdle, Word Cat Editorial Services
Copyeditor and Proofreader:	Lynette M. Smith, All My Best
Book Cover and Interior Designer:	Elena Reznikova, DTPerfect
Publisher:	Imagine a More Promising Future Publishing
	ImagineAMorePromisingFuture.com

ISBN (hardcover):	978-1-954912-04-5
ISBN (paperback):	978-1-954912-06-9
ISBN (eBook):	978-1-954912-05-2
ISBN (audiobook):	978-1-954912-07-6

Library of Congress Control Number: 2022912904

Contact the author at
ImagineAMorePromisingFuture.com

Contents

Preface vii

Introduction: Purpose

Educating the Whole Student: How Teacher Expertise
Affects Student Outcomes 3
It Begins on Day One 3
Supporting the Whole Teacher 5

Part 1: Problems

Chapter 1: Root Problems 11
  Failed Leadership 11
  School Leadership Impacts the Well-Being of a School's Culture 13
  Solution: Ensure Compatibility 15
  Disconnect Between Policymakers and Classroom Realities .. 16
  How Social Stigmas Influence School Budgets 20
  The Failure to Replicate Promising Education Reforms 21
  Education Reform Pioneers Who Succeeded 22

Chapter 2: Symptoms 26
  Run-Down Schools 26
  School Staff in Crisis 27
  The Precarious Position of First-Year Teachers 27
  How Systemically Failing School Culture Impedes Teachers' Success ... 30
  Working Toward a Solution 32
  Chronic Understaffing and Overcrowding: An Untenable Situation .. 34
  Exodus of Experienced Leaders 37

Chapter 3: How Problems Affect Students 39
  The Weight of Teacher Turnover 39
  Why Each Student Must Be Seen as a Whole Person 40

Part 2:
Transformational Staffing Model— Missing Links Unmasked

Chapter 4: Overview of Transformational Staffing Model 47
   School-Based Professional Development Specialists 47
   *Resources Needed to Cultivate Exceptional Classrooms:
A Reconstructed Teacher Training Paradigm* 49
   *Higher Education's Role in Preparing New Cohort of
Professional Specialists* 50
   Addressing Instructional Gap Impediments 52
   Understanding the Limits of Standardized Assessments 53
   Making Cognitive Development a Priority 54
   The Transformational Staffing Model in Action 57
   Benefits for New Teachers 57
   *Honoring Veteran Teachers' Experience and Empowering
Them Further* 60
   Working Toward Measurable Outcomes 62
   Best Evidence: Students Master Learning 64
   Educational Excellence Links Quality Teaching to Student Learning ... 64
   *How We Ensure Attainment of Improved Professional
Performance Outcomes* 66
   The Exceptional Classroom Plan 68

Chapter 5: Content Specialist 70
   Content Instruction Today 70
   Bridging the Gap with Content Specialists 72

**Chapter 6: Understanding the Convergence of Content
and Instruction** 75

Chapter 7: Instructional Support Specialist 80
   A Personal Journey of Learning Deficiencies 80
   Self-Taught Solutions to Advance My Education 81
   Learning Skills Essential for Learning Success 83
   Contemporary Practices in Today's Lesson Plans 85
   Merging Cultural Identity with Instruction 85
   *Instructional Support Specialists Can Solve Jigsaw Puzzle:
Aligning Standards with Lessons* 87
   Demystifying Standards to Allow Transparency for Students 89
   Why We Should Refrain from Predetermining Students' Levels of Ability ... 89
   Student Learning Profiles Should Determine Instructional Resources 90

Contents

Chapter 8: Differentiating Technology Maintenance from Computer Literacy 92
   Consequences of Inadequate Computer Science Education 93
   Making the Case for a Technology Curriculum and Instruction Specialist.................................... 94
   Evolution of Digital Footprints in and Beyond Schools 97

Chapter 9: Classroom Management Specialist 99
   An Overview.. 99
   Students Want to Know What Goals to Aspire to Achieve and How to Achieve Them..................................... 101
   What All Teachers Have in Common 105
   Setting Expectations Is Key to Well-Managed Classrooms........ 105
   Students Are Environmentalists 106
   Why Students Owe Teachers No Favors 108
   Students Dispensing M&M's 108
   What if What You Said Didn't Matter Because of How It Was Said 109
   Detecting Fissures...................................... 110
   The Contagiousness of Generosity 111
   Why New Teachers Never Need to Apologize 113
   The Connection Between a Student's Self-Esteem and Class Culture . 114
   The Challenge of Reframing How Students Perceive and Respond to Errors................................... 117
   Rescuing Students Who Have Encountered Learning Challenges 120
   Extending Courtesy Beyond Their First Day.................. 121

Chapter 10: Inclusion Support Specialist..................... 124
   How to Cultivate Socially Appropriate Habits 124
   Strengthening Inclusion Practices in General Education Classrooms . 125
   How We Include the Broad Spectrum of Student Populations...... 127

Chapter 11: Academic Achievement Specialist................ 130
   Schools Need Academic Achievement Specialists 130
   Why Achieving Mastery Should Be the Benchmark for All Students . 130
   What Will Be Seen When We Widen the Educational Lens 131
   The Need to Broaden Our Awareness....................... 132
   Bringing to Fruition the Goal of Achieving Proficiency 132
   Someone Who Can Transform Data into a Student Performance Plan...................................... 133

Chapter 12: **The Transformative Staffing Model in Action** 135
    Adding Instructional Efficacy to the Teaching Paradigm 136
    *Strengthening Instruction by Adding the Why to Prevent
    Learning Deficiencies* 137

Part 3: Continuation of Instruction

Chapter 13: **Ensuring Exceptional Classrooms During Crises** ... 145
    *Education in the Time of COVID: The Domino Effect
    of School Closures During the Pandemic* 145
    Continuation of Education Plan 148
    *Lessons Learned About the Importance of Technology
    in the Classroom* 151
    Satellite Classroom Networks 152
    Anticipation of Satellite Classroom Concerns 156
    Preparing Students for Satellite Classrooms and Remote Learning ... 157
    Mobility of New Professional Development Resources 159
    Delivering Quality Education Across All Platforms 161

Chapter 14: **Emotional/Mental Health and the Continuation
of Instruction** 163
    Preventing Health Insecurity Gaps 163
    A New Model of Counseling 164

Conclusion 169

Appendix:
Roles and Responsibilities of Professional Development Specialists

Overview 173
Content Specialist 176
Instructional Support Specialist 179
Classroom Management Specialist 182
Inclusion Support Specialist 187
Academic Achievement Specialist 191

Acknowledgments 197
About the Author 199

Preface

AMERICA'S EDUCATION SYSTEM IS IN CRISIS. OUR TEACHING workforce is shrinking and shows no signs of reversing course. Predictably, the most detrimentally impacted are students. The constant flow of educators leaving schools further hinders student performance outcomes in public schools across poor and minority communities, which already endure so many disadvantages. School districts are experiencing a real "Break Glass in Case of Emergency" moment as the urgent demand for teachers to fill positions across most states increases at an alarming rate. Many people will attribute the mass departure to the COVID-19 pandemic. While the pandemic has accelerated the pace of current teacher departures, our national teaching shortage actually began in the years preceding COVID. Both the prolonged and recent departures have something in common at their core: an erosion of trust.

COVID exacerbated and intensified the widespread exit of teachers, but it has revealed other fissures in our public education system. Teaching shortages were forecasted several years ago when enrollment in college teaching programs saw significant declines in students interested in pursuing a career in teaching. When teachers employed in public schools began to leave the profession, there simply were not enough trained professionals available to replace them. As the volume of early departures increased, many districts were caught by surprise. Instead of paying attention to the earliest signals foreshadowing early retirements and taking proactive measures to prevent mass exoduses, districts suddenly find themselves reacting. Regrettably, there seems to be little interest in determining the causes for the departures. *Burnout* is among the most common reasons teachers will openly admit to contributing to their decision to quit.

Burnout, which is a mental, emotional, and physical health issue, can take many forms. Over-exhaustion and stress are contributors. Then the arrival of a health pandemic caused so much more uncertainty that massive numbers of teachers chose to not return to work when schools reopened. Having previously experienced being ignored when trying to convey signs of distress related to poor working conditions, many teachers wondered how they could possibly entrust those same leaders with critical life decisions. Many existing fissures expose the level of erosion of trust, and the arrival of an unprecedented health crisis widened the chasm even further. Initially, teachers and families truly wanted and needed to be able to trust the judgment of those responsible for their personal health and well-being. Yet they sensed that decisions for reopening schools for in-person learning had more to do with a desire to rescue the economy, which needed students back in school so parents, who are among the nation's highest number of employees, could return to work. Teachers and parents became skeptical about assurances that conditions were safe. Such skepticism resulted in significant spikes in staffing shortages during school reopenings because teachers and other staff members diligently kept track of the number of hospitalizations and the rising death rates in their communities. They saw that, despite the data, plans to reopen schools were proceeding.

Though school districts pledged to unequivocally hold every school, without exception, to the absolute highest safety protocol standards, these promises fell short in schools with nonworking—and in some cases nonexistent—HVAC systems. Shortages of testing kits to honor rapid-testing promises, along with poorly managed contact-tracing efforts, added to the mistrust. Those issues were then compounded by the lack of careful monitoring to track COVID's presence within schools. That was an especially problematic misstep.

Even more tragic were the measures some school districts took to blatantly disguise or cover up any information that contradicted their messaging. Once teachers, students, and family members began to fall sick with COVID, members of the community discovered they could no longer trust what they were being told. The decision to contradict the actual data, *which was also imperfect*, was, for teachers and families, more evidence of a failure in leadership. For many educators, the increasing misrepresentations about the status of COVID infections in their communities, and eventually into their schools, significantly spiked their level of mistrust. Predictably, more teacher departures were inevitable.

Teacher salaries have long been among the lowest among many professions, and were another reason high numbers of teachers were exiting the profession. Across many states, salaries are still very low; this holds little to no appeal for college students who seek a profession that offers more than incomes not even high enough to keep up with the cost of living while repaying astronomically high student loans. Reversing the current trajectory of low enrollment rates in college teaching programs and the continued flow of early teacher departures from classrooms is not only a salary issue but a lack-of-school-based-resources issue. Both are directly tied to underfunded school budgets. Increased funding at the school level is the catalyst needed to retain teachers and increase enrollment in college teacher training programs.

Preface

Over the years, not only did the continued cycle of budget cuts for public schools contribute to teachers' earning low incomes, but the reduced budgets forced those who remained in schools to take on additional responsibilities with little to no support. Across many communities, news of budget cuts is made public; but rarely is the public informed about the consequences of those cuts. Decreases in school budgets often cause a reduction in staff members. When the number of students enrolled either stays the same or increases, the process of redistributing students among the remaining staff members is beyond burdensome. Inheriting more students results in filling classrooms beyond their capacity and disrupts the entire educational eco-system in classrooms. To be clear, staff reductions and overpopulated classrooms contributed to downgrading the quality of instruction many years prior to COVID. Once the pandemic arrived on the doorstep of every school, it brought more uncertainty and unleashed widespread health insecurity. Expecting already overworked and underappreciated school staff to rely on federal and district leaders to be truthful and transparent when announcing assurances related to pandemic safety protocols left many feeling even more dubious. In essence, those in charge of administering inadequate school budgets, that reflected how poorly teachers were valued, were now responsible for ensuring the health of students, teachers, and their family members at a moment when there was little margin for error.

Despite these challenges, our public education system remains one of the foundational pillars our society relies on to educate students. The arrival of COVID may have exacerbated the failures of our public education system, but those failures have been in need of our attention over the span of many decades. The pervasive educational disparities evident in student performance outcomes in poor communities are because of decreasing school budgets, increased teacher departures, and low student enrollment in college teaching programs. But the overarching disparity is the ongoing lack of respect for America's teaching profession. By way of example, let's look at another pervasive movement that shows even further evidence of a lack of respect for teachers. States unable to keep pace with the volume of teacher departures are deploying measures that will irreparably harm our education system. State leaders are replacing trained licensed professionals with unlicensed and unqualified adults for teaching positions in classrooms. Not only is it a disastrous decision, but it further devalues the teaching profession. However, there is one beneficiary of the current cycle of staffing shortages resulting in the hiring of citizens without the prerequisite professional license: the conditions for eroding trust in our public education system are serving the interests of those who have long pined for the opportunity to privatize our education system. Proponents of expanding school choice and voucher programs are poised to seize any opportunity to increase the presence of charter schools. The recent hiring of unlicensed adults to drive school buses, work in cafeterias, or take over teaching positions, where the only qualification required is *availability*, helps to fuel expectations of an inevitable collapse. Most frightening is the absolute disregard for student safety. But irresponsible measures that deny students the right to receive an education from non-credentialed staff members allowed to pose as teachers ought to outrage everyone. Are we really willing to tolerate exchanging instruction with conditions that resemble highly populated study halls?

Dismissing previous qualifications and setting aside state and federal licensing requirements, in order to allow the casual replacement of skilled teachers with unqualified staff members, is a sign that schools will likely become day-care facilities that require only minimal instruction and learning. We should all be highly concerned at this moment, but not totally shocked. Efforts to privatize our public education system have been successful across many communities over the past few decades. When politicians overtake the authority of superintendents and entire school departments, while being courted by corporations invested in the expansion of school choice, the timing of those decisions is not coincidental. Incentives offered to democratic and republican politicians have proven to be quite a persuasive tactic.

The recent renewed interest in increasing charter schools in urban communities across the country has had a chilling effect on communities who were once promised, by those running for office, that public schools would never be abandoned. More specifically, reassurances included explicit commitments to improve schools, prevent them from closing, and under no circumstances allow an expansion in the number of charter schools in their city. Promises quickly lost credibility when schools' annual budgets continued to decline. Shrinking budgets all but ensured educational inequities would continue, causing academic achievement gaps to widen further. All of the broken promises, combined with the lack of investments in measures to improve the educational fortunes of poor and predominantly minority communities, have allowed the political narratives of "failing public schools" to gather more steam in the hopes of convincing the public that charter schools and school choice are the only remaining choice.

The existence of public charter schools has been a bit of a conundrum. Many years ago, when I first heard about charter schools, my opinion revolved around a belief that any school successful in providing quality education with measurably verifiable results was worthy of being supported. Today I hold in very high regard some charter schools that have certifiably been able to prove a history of having achieved high academic standards. Regrettably, the inequitable funding formula, where charter schools have evolved at the expense of public schools, which can least afford to incur additional financial loss, resulted in charter schools' coming at a high cost to public schools. The funding model used by federal and state leaders in the departments of education to bolster student enrollment in charter schools was unfair. Students unenrolled in public schools and transferred into charter schools had the same level of per-pupil allocated funds transferred with them. The drop in enrollment in public schools significantly depleted their school budgets. Basically, it seemed the funding allocation process relied on a practice of robbing poor Peter to pay economically well-off Paul. But the real insult to injury was being promised by the state that the equivalent of funds lost due to student transfers would be fully or partially refunded to school districts. In many communities, that promise was never fulfilled.

There has been a recent emergence of another perspective shared by a segment of our population: those who see the education delivered in public schools as an infringement on the rights of parents. While I wholeheartedly agree that parents ought to be included in the educational process of their children, I have concerns about extreme points of view expressing displeasure with issues related to inclusion and celebration of our nation's pluralism. In fact, their attempts to replace factual content in school curriculums prevents me from regarding their demands as rational or in any way helpful in efforts to identify and address disparities in our education system. What they propose will only serve to widen the disparities. And it feels intentional.

The makeup of some school board candidates, in strong support of fringe ideology that does not remotely represent quality educational policies, is adding fuel to the level of mistrust in our public education system. If federal funding is the primary source of public school budgets, it seems the government should use its oversight authority to review new standards and mandates to ensure that efforts to eradicate legitimate content from schoolbooks and overthrow school policies that support equity for all students do not succeed. Government funds have been withheld from organizations that are in non-compliance with regulations that were made explicitly clear. Public schools are the property of the federal government, and so too should be the policies inside of all public schools funded by the government.

Ongoing verbal, physical, and emotional abuse and threats endured by schools' staff and leaders are also causing more departures. The turmoil incited by adults harboring groundless grievances against government agencies has found its way to the doorsteps of our public schools in several regions. What I find most confounding is the absence of any effort by government officials to push back and prevent this group of education obstructionists from entering schools. To combat recent attempts to undermine our public education system, such initiatives as federal government intervention and oversight must be undertaken to ensure the protection of current teachers and staff members, whom we need to remain in the profession. Students are already learning to live with the uncertainty of their personal safety inside of schools; how much more pain should be inflicted on them? Communities with constituents who fervently disagree with policies and freely choose how they will communicate their displeasure are cultivating bullying and intimidation tactics with impunity; while other populations, who do less or may not be guilty of anything, are subjected to harsher responses.

In addition to guaranteeing the protection of school staff, students, and family members, there are other immediate and pragmatic steps we can and should consider taking, right away, to retain teachers and other staff members. Since teachers are so central to preserving educational standards, it makes sense to focus on what they need to convince them to remain in classrooms. Now is a great time to start rethinking how we value and express our appreciation to members of the teaching profession. One idea to convey how much we value what they do for America's children is to extend Teacher Appreciation Day throughout the entire school year. What would make it more meaningful is to align proclamations of appreciation with evidence proving how much their efforts are held in high esteem. Raises in salary may entice more teachers to remain in the profession. In addition to increasing salaries, their student loan debts should be forgiven. Loan debt forgiveness and higher teaching salaries will also incentivize more college students to enroll in teaching programs. Future generations of trained and fully qualified educators will be needed to replace those who retire, as well the current crop of untrained and unlicensed recruits occupying teaching positions in schools in some states.

Another idea to convey how much we value a teacher's service is to direct our attention to their professional aspirations of making a difference in the lives of their students. Their ability to make a meaningful difference in the lives of their students has got to translate into actionable steps that result in strengthening the quality of instruction they plan and deliver each day. Our education system can design a professional development model designating resources to advance the professional growth of teachers. The actionable steps in this book are framed around the mission every teacher intended to achieve when they initially chose a career in teaching: to cultivate classroom cultures that enable all students to learn.

Cultivating Exceptional Classrooms envisions ways to elevate teacher success and prevent burnout. The measures proposed for helping teachers cultivate exceptional classrooms would greatly benefit from a united group of advocates in favor of efforts to rejuvenate our investment in public education. I believe it starts with recognizing the real value of those who worked to earn college degrees, met the necessary qualifications required for a teaching license, and then dedicated themselves to a career of constantly giving. Because of our failure to recognize and appreciate the real value of public-school teachers, conditions have continued to deteriorate further, making it impossible for many teachers and other school staff members to remain in the profession. Their ambivalence about their decision to leave is sincere. It is often evident in the tears that flow while they carry packed boxes from their classroom to their car.

It is the dedicated teachers—those who tirelessly give of themselves on behalf of their students—who led me to conclude that now is the time to bring awareness about the extensive demands placed on school staff members. Staffing shortages are leading to overpopulated classrooms. Overpopulated classrooms create conditions less conducive to teaching and learning. I may sound like a bit of an alarmist, but I do wonder: how many of us are truly aware that our public education system may be teetering on the verge of collapse across many low-income communities?

We hear, but do not seem to take seriously, threats of public schools across poor urban and rural communities being taken over by corporations interested in expanding privatization of our education system. Those of us advocating for our national government to retain control of our public education system have to create a movement to improve our public education system, and make it worthy of saving. Changes are needed to justify why it should remain under the auspices of our national government. Those changes may also prove to be our best chance of replacing educational policies that have contributed to our current predicament in which underperforming schools produce underwhelming numbers of highly educated students.

Enhancing the quality of education is not just the responsibility of teachers; it belongs to all of us. We can insist schools are allocated budgets necessary to fund professional development resources; but let's make certain they are directed at the classroom level. It is essential that all professional development resources are aligned with today's realities and the responsibilities teachers perform in classrooms.

This preface began with a discussion about factors contributing to an erosion of trust that has resulted in increasing numbers of teacher departures. Sadly, if we are unable to replace qualified and trained teaching professionals with other qualified professionals, confidence in our public schools will erode even further, and that will also clear the way for expansion of charter schools. The choice between sending your child to a place that provides an education versus facilities replacing qualified teachers with *available* adults capable of just supervising them may eventually be the real, and only, *school choice* model of the 21st century.

It is unacceptable to educate our kids in public schools that lack professionally trained and qualified teachers. The lasting impact of remote learning for many students currently enrolled in overcrowded classrooms supervised by unlicensed adults will make recovering lost learning time unlikely. Similar to the aftermath of citizens who recovered from the virus but now suffer from long-haul symptoms, for so many children whose education was paused during remote learning, the addition of unqualified staff in schools will increase the lapse of instructional time and further jeopardize the students' chances of recovering the education they are being denied.

Introduction: Purpose

Educating the Whole Student:
How Teacher Expertise Affects Student Outcomes

Q UALIFIED, SKILLED TEACHERS ARE THE FOUNDATION OF STUDENT success in the classroom. Their level of education is critical and consequential to the broad range of responsibilities required to educate their students. Acquainting readers about each of the labor-intensive and arduous responsibilities required of teachers is next to impossible. Without the proper training and guidance, teachers are enormously challenged in the responsibility of managing a diverse population of students. In spite of their strong determination to succeed, many first-year teachers are capable but inadequately equipped to meet this challenge on their own.

It Begins on Day One

In the early days of the start of a new school year, orienting students to class routines, policies, schedules, and expectations generally feels familiar. The rituals associated with the start of a new school year bring about a feeling of comfort for most students. The fact that most schools have had similar routines in place for years, across all grade levels, helps students predict expectations at the start of each school year; it makes for a seamless transition from one grade to the next. In fact, their familiarity with the first-day-of-school rituals, generally contributes to their excitement and eagerness to be back in school. Appearing ready for another year of instruction at a new grade level is a socially conditioned response. For example, fifth grade students who have attended the same school since kindergarten have learned what to expect in previous years. Upon their arrival they settle in and take on a posture of compliance. The calm and relaxed presence of students familiar with opening day routines contributes to the appearance of a stable school and classroom culture.

However, after the initial days of a rather smooth beginning, which many teachers refer to as *the honeymoon period,* the shift to instruction is where they notice the emergence of how truly diverse and varied students' performance levels differ from one another. Differing, too, are the levels of confidence among students in what initially appeared to be a uniform population ready to learn. Because students experience the process of learning differently, the 20 to 25 seats filled on day one will eventually reveal the presence of 20 to 25 different learning profiles.

When the agenda shifts from orientation about policies, teacher expectations, and other non-academic activities to instruction, teachers are often perplexed by the changes that come over their students. Those who learn more quickly are excited when their classroom culture finally shifts from social orientation about class policies and routines to instruction. However, for students who struggle with learning, it can be terrifying to shift from having time to get socially acclimated—for many, their strongest asset—to instruction.

Disruption to a student's social comfort zone can cause some to retreat and reemerge as an entirely different person from the one who previously appeared quite friendly and compliant. Reemerged personas can come in many different behavioral forms, including shyness, inability to stay focused, excessive talkativeness, frequent distractability, or clowning activity. Yet schools often overlook the link between academic instruction and the sudden manifestation of distracting behaviors. Changes in behavior by students who previously experienced academic failure can elicit signs of fear and insecurity about having to experience another year of doing poorly in a particular subject or multiple subjects.

Why haven't we yet figured out behaviors that are potentially a manifestation of learning frustrations, which can unleash subtle or dramatically different behaviors from students who once appeared so socially well-adjusted and willing to abide by classroom policies? It's puzzling. Let's not make the mistake of judging and then labeling these students as something other than what they initially appeared to be in the beginning of the school year. Instead, for their sake, let's pause and ask, "What could have triggered the change in attitude and behaviors?"

If the change can be traced directly to the cultural shift of a classroom, from focusing on orienting students regarding class routines and social norms, to instruction, we might discover that our education system is built on a few erroneous assumptions related to grouping students homogeneously. While grouping same-age students together for reasons related to social development, our public education system seemed to have relied on the cookie-cutter belief that same-age groupings meant we could conveniently ignore the diverse range of learners performing at different levels.

It's important to acknowledge that the students who started the school year appearing so well-adjusted and socially together are still the same people, if we can educate them without treading on their individual comfort zone. Student fragility that emerges in school but nowhere else in a student's life outside of school is likely induced by the experience of educational frustration; and for some it can be the equivalent to their third rail. Similar to the ordinary-looking but highly dangerous rail associated along train tracks we've all been forewarned to never come into contact with, experiencing academic failure can also be frighteningly perilous for many students.

For students experiencing learning frustrations, restoring their belief in their ability to learn can be achieved by reversing their feeling of failure and teaching them *how* to learn. *Welcome to the core mission of this book.* To achieve that mission, we must focus on supporting the most essential resource of each classroom: the teacher.

Supporting the Whole Teacher

If schools want to succeed in educating the whole student, that process has to start with attending to the professional development of their teachers across the multiple areas of responsibility needed to educate and manage their classrooms. I'm advocating for professional development resources for teachers that will shift them from struggling to survive to thriving and achieving their maximum potential—and that of their students.

Symbolically, all topics in this book represent a *lifejacket* intended to support teachers, whose real value is yet to be fully acknowledged and appreciated. Sharing the missing links to help teachers cultivate exceptional classrooms is the lifejacket schools have needed to advance the professional skills of those responsible for educating students. This particular lifejacket contains professional resources that will significantly impact every teacher's professional competency in areas linked with their responsibilities in their classrooms. A comprehensive professional development model based entirely on advancing the professional skills of teachers at the classroom level will lead to the emergence of pedagogical standards and practices demonstrating that teachers are capable of cultivating exceptional classrooms. The professional development model I propose examines key areas that, on the surface, appear to be about a single issue. But when we delve deeper into the conditions of classroom life, we discover the interconnected and complex relationship between each of the areas.

It is understood that educating all students is tied to a teacher's classroom-management practices. On the surface, references to managing a classroom usually mean class routines, policy enforcement, addressing of rule infractions, and teaching of lessons. But one of the essential strategies for successfully managing a class is to recognize the value of creating accessible pathways enabling students to connect with instruction. The process of capturing student interest in lessons from the very beginning is what ignites a willingness to get on board. When students feel fully included and capable at the start of lessons, they are more apt to tolerate challenges. The key is to design welcoming points of entry when launching each lesson. Engaging every student by using investigative techniques that invite curiosity or exploration is less intimidating. Opportunities for self-discovery, or multi-step scavenger hunts with helpful hints to guide them through a process that leads them to obtaining the correct answer, are ways teachers can establish comfort at the start of every lesson.

The task in cultivating conditions for exceptional classrooms is to build the confidence of students who have experienced learning frustration. Student interest in lessons can help restore a student's confidence. That matters because if they feel confident, they will be motivated to attend school. Improving a student's desire to want to attend school comes from the quality of instruction they receive, which influences how they experience education. Understanding the intricacies of lesson planning as a means of elevating student interest in learning, which is dependent on their level of comfort in participating and bolsters their confidence, greatly influences classroom management. Schools can accelerate the professional growth of teachers in many key areas directly connected with educating students, by establishing school-level professional development support to help teachers become familiar with the intricate process of how to plan and jump-start lessons designed to ensure the full participation of all students, as a means of managing their class.

Our education system often invests resources that sometimes make a difference along the fringes—providing new books, or partnering with corporations that generously donate new equipment for computer labs. All such efforts are needed and appreciated. *But we cannot serve the best interests of students without directing resources to school staff and classroom teachers.* If we want to effectively address academic performance outcomes in every class, let's start by redirecting our focus of education reform where it is needed most: at the nucleus of our education system, inside classrooms. What type and quality of resources are needed to improve the overall education happening inside of classrooms? If we are to improve conditions for learning, the resources provided must be aligned with the realities of the daily challenges teachers and staff members encounter at the school level.

One of many reasons why this book advocates for an infusion of professional development and other resources specifically for teachers and other school staff members, is to close numerous informational gaps. The example of how accessible entry points at the start of lessons can be valuable in managing a classroom is not widely known among first-year teachers. Teachers were also never adequately trained in recognizing learning gaps or useful instructional remedies to address the root causes. If teachers were never informed about how instruction and learning practices impact classroom culture, it seems unfair to hold them accountable. But we do. When students earn failing grades, we never consider whether their grades reflect learning gaps due to challenges students have with learning, or if they are due to gaps in instruction. There are many unknowns regarding the quality and quantity of education students receive. Disparities in student performances may be related not only to the absence of content never taught but also to method of instruction used. Whether due to content not being covered or method of instruction being inadequate, both are obstacles to a student's ability to receive a comprehensive education.

Students who are denied a comprehensive education are at an unfair disadvantage. They may perform poorly on standardized tests because the assessments cover a broad spectrum of content topics. The scores reflecting degree of learning proficiency lack any opportunity to identify reasons for poor performance in any portion of the tests. There are no boxes to check, to indicate whether the questions were answered as they were, due to lack of familiarity of topics because they were not covered in lessons. The *unsatisfactory* category indicating level of performance outcome achieved is indisputable and, unfortunately, final.

The range of benefits to students when teachers learn ways to improve their teaching practices includes reducing students' fear of failure, particularly when taking standardized tests. Preventing learning insecurity and educational fragility is possible. Students' self-esteem is heightened when teaching practices are improved so that students experience success with learning. As students' self-confidence grows, they internalize the belief in their ability to learn, which contributes to sustainable periods of academic achievement. The cycles of success will help students conquer the insecurities and apprehensions so many currently experience while getting ready to go to school each day. What once felt insurmountable to students lagging behind and left to wonder if they even possessed the ability to succeed in school, will *finally* be replaced with a sense of certainty about their ability to learn.

In the following chapters, we'll explore the root causes that perpetuate dysfunction in many of our schools, as well as the observable problems that grow from these roots. We will also identify the degree to which the dysfunction hinders student learning and how it impedes students from advancing their education. *Cultivating Exceptional Classrooms* is intended not only to unmask missing links in achieving quality education but also to help readers comprehend the factors contributing to the inequities in our public education system that have prevented generations of students from achieving their true learning potential.

Part 1:
Problems

CHAPTER 1

Root Problems

A S AN EDUCATOR WITH EXTENSIVE TEACHING, CONSULTING, and leadership experience, and as someone who cares deeply about students, I've given much thought to the patterns of dysfunction I've observed over the years. In my experience, three intertwined and recurring problems lie at the root of chronically underperforming schools: a fundamental lack of qualified leadership at the district and/ or school level, a disconnect in understanding the purpose of education between uninformed policymakers and qualified educators at the school level, and grossly inadequate budgets.

Failed Leadership

Capable leadership is one of the hallmarks of school cultures that thrive. In the school environment, this means that the leader is truly qualified for the position, treats staff with respect, and understands the importance of leading by example. When these attributes are present, their staff members can focus on teaching students without being concerned about how to survive tumultuous circumstances that occasionally occur in school environments.

Education is a noble and phenomenal profession when it rewards competent and authentically qualified professionals. Unfortunately, it has a propensity to sometimes reward mediocrity or allow those unworthy of the profession to *fail up*. Currently, there is no national registry that tracks educator performance relative to metrics of competency or those identified as not having satisfactorily met professional standards. Too often, those who earn poor performance evaluations in previous positions manage to hopscotch from one position to a higher one, which leads to having unqualified people in positions of leadership. Just as students must demonstrate proficiency in order to attain the next grade level, we need a national system for tracking and objectively verifying educator competency for all leadership positions.

Education is a highly magnetic field that attracts its share of wannabe leaders at all levels. When unqualified or unproven individuals ascend to influential positions in districts and schools, it can have a disastrous effect on staff morale and student performance outcomes. But how do they get hired?

The gift of cosmetically packaging oneself in preparation for an interview is how many get a foothold in doors they may not be qualified to enter. Part of the cosmetic packaging process extends to embellished résumés as well as overall physical presentation. Candidates with truly good interview skills often impress selection committees with their well-rehearsed communication style that enhances their social interaction skills. Unfortunately, some committee members feel these superficial qualities are sufficient standards for determining whether candidates possess the necessary attributes for leadership. But these surface qualities do not indicate the true qualifications needed to do the job well.

If we are to ensure we are bringing the most qualified candidates into the education profession, a more rigorous and less subjective interview process is imperative. Interview-committee members may also need to add more steps to the process of verifying candidates' references. Perhaps delving a bit deeper in the vetting process might reveal why, in some cases, references seem overly enthusiastic during inquiries about the candidate.

It takes skill and judgment to discern the difference between credibly competent applicants and those who sprinkle mistruths in their less-than-honorable résumés. While committee members hope to hear confirmation of prospective leaders' abilities, they need to weigh references judiciously. Incompetent leaders receiving attaboy or attagirl pats on the back from colleagues who happily spoke highly of them might be a cause for concern. Subordinates tired of succumbing to the whims of incompetent managers or education leaders can be quite willing to exaggerate about the "exceptional" qualifications of those whom they have waited a long time to be rid of. Praise from co-workers bolstering someone's credentials might seem promising at face value, but what if it has more to do with their growing impatience as they wait for any opportunity to help that person exit from their current position?

Competent colleagues who are forced to work with far-less-qualified people in any position, but particularly in leadership roles, eventually become so desperate to find a way to move on from those individuals that they may undertake their own job searches. However, rumors about unqualified leaders seeking a new position elsewhere, may elevate the hopes of colleagues eager for their leader to move on. Unfortunately, the opportunity to aid the exit of incompetent leaders can make co-workers willing to stoop to tactics that result in another organization's inheriting the leader's incompetency. Eager to do whatever they can to help the transition happen, co-workers or those in higher positions are so desperate to be rid of someone that they will substitute the candidate's true qualities with mythically glowing attributes. This really hurts the integrity of our education system.

As disturbing as this last-ditch measure may be, it's important to recognize that such decisions are often strategically calibrated moves of last resort used by some staff, only after they've reported their concerns to human resources. Quite often, principals, teachers and staff who try to work within the chain of command to address failures of leadership at the school or district level face pushback from superiors or others in high-ranking positions. This creates an awkward situation for the whistleblower and further erodes morale.

When staff choose to report incidents worthy of investigation and then see no action taken, they can be left with a sinking feeling that the person being reported may have personal connections to those in the upper echelon of the organization. The fear of consequences boomeranging back to those filing legitimate complaints is quite common in education, where personal friendships are at a premium and supersede qualifications on one's résumé. (Again, this culture of subjective preferential treatment plays out on many levels within our education system.)

Regardless of the cause, changes in leadership are both inevitable and consequential. While change is challenging at any time, it's much more so when qualified, successful school leaders are replaced with incompetent administrators who lack experience and skill. These shifts can have a cascading effect within schools; and as difficult as it is for teachers and staff, students are the ones who have the most to lose.

Veteran teachers who have worked with more than one school leader understand how the cycle of administrative changes shifts the equilibrium of a classroom's culture. In many cases, these teachers have established reputations through years of earning the trust of school principals and the respect of parents. When less-qualified leaders enact new policies, schedules, and grade and course assignments, replacing practices that have operated well under previous leaders, these veteran teachers must learn how to balance their independence (and the success of their students) with school and district expectations.

School Leadership Impacts the Well-Being of a School's Culture

Unfortunately, the change in standards isn't just a high-level administrative shift; the revolving door of school and district leaders' coming and going directly impacts students in the classroom. This is particularly problematic when unqualified educators are brought in to replace highly competent leaders with successful track records. The system of replacing qualified leaders reminds us of what Forrest stated in the movie, *Forrest Gump*: "Life is like a box of chocolates. You never know what you're going to get." Is this what we want from our education system?

When we allow weak leaders to shape school culture, it can undo years of success and relationship building. Undoubtedly, some changes may be needed, and qualified administrators must implement them with skill and judgment; but teachers are quick to detect the havoc that's created when pragmatic policies and routines that have worked for years are switched out for less effective policies that seem to have no real basis for existing other than being what the new school leader wants.

If teachers who are used to being trusted and worthy of autonomy start to feel constricted by policies that erode a school's culture, classroom doors that used to remain open will frequently be closed. This small change signals the teachers' intention to reclaim their autonomy. It's basically a *keep away* plan. When new policies lead to a decline in trust in a leader's ability to operationally manage a school, the evidence is often found in how quickly an entire school becomes untethered from longstanding procedures due to lack of or ineffective enforcement of any policies. That spurs a quick erosion of faith in leaders who then respond with further retaliatory measures in the form of proclamations described as measures intended to support the mission of achieving a culture of "academic success." Experienced staff members are quite adept at detecting the real reasons for the new measures, which they know will predictably further the erosion of the school's culture.

Whatever occurs inside of schools, one significant bellwether of a school's culture in a state of decline is the palpable presence of dampened enthusiasm felt among the majority of staff. Students are among the first to notice the gradual erosion. The experience can be so disconcerting that they begin to convey their concerns to family members. If the person is a newly selected school leader, most people are naturally inclined to wait and see, or at least give them a chance. Opportunities to take measures to right the ship and produce favorable outcomes are generally welcomed and appreciated by staff members when the leader is less concerned about the need to save face and protect his or her reputation, and instead reaches out to their staff to extend an olive branch and inquire about what can be done to press a reset button. Leaders with integrity are not afraid to invite dialog with staff members to hear their perspective about what is causing an erosion of their trust and how they can collectively work to improve the conditions. That is the profile of leaders who arrive and, despite having the best of intentions, make erroneous decisions but are willing to address and correct those decisions for the good of their school's culture and the students they remain committed to serve.

In truth, there are school leaders who have summoned the courage to listen to and learn from experienced staff members and then proceed to make changes that restored their faith in one another. Rarely do we see such opportunities to reverse the trajectory of a school's culture teetering on the verge of decline, undertaken in a dignified manner and through humane actions of grace. Competent leaders willing to work collaboratively with their staff who are devoted to their school's cultural well-being are to be commended. When school leaders are selected at the district level, or when the selected candidate is imposed on the school by district leaders and then proves not to be a "good" or "compatible" fit, the school is stuck in a quagmire. Candidates selected at the district level may arrive with an agenda that is counterintuitive and undermines the mission of the school. When such leaders arrive with new policies, show no willingness to be flexible, and make it abundantly clear that all decisions made at the top are non-negotiable, these are warning signs that this particular person is not a good fit to the school's culture.

Solution: Ensure Compatibility

One viable way to prevent the hiring of leadership candidates who may not fit a school's culture is to change the interview and hiring process. Let's revisit the hiring process for new school leaders. The current standard practice of assembling an interview committee includes recruiting one or more staff members. It is a token gesture. Some staff participants are under the false impression that their presence will represent all points of view of the entire staff. Others are under no such illusion. Veteran teachers who are selected are not flattered. Those who eventually get to "yes" may willingly volunteer, but most finally give in to the relentless begging from a designated committee leader. Desperate to meet the composition standards school districts make unequivocally clear, the objective is to recruit members that represent the diversity of the school's community. Those assembled must represent a demographic portrait capable of withstanding accusations of inequity and unfairness.

Designated leaders of interview committees are enormously relieved when the recruitment process has been completed and they can check off the box listing recruitment as one of the tasks required for assembling what the district deemed as a *fair representation of constituents*. The presence of a few staff members is not an accurate microcosm of an entire staff's points of view; there is no one cohesive or unifying point of view among a diverse staff. Just like classrooms that are populated with students representing diverse learning profiles, levels of performance, opinions, and a range of other issues that matter across a very broad spectrum of areas, no two staff members—let alone an entire staff—think alike.

The current model prevents candidates the opportunity to get a broader and more accurate representation about the school. Every school interview process should incorporate a meet-and-greet session that enables candidates who qualify as one of the finalists to sit with the entire staff to hear their perspectives about what they hope the new leader can and will do to build on the school's successes and work with them to address areas in need of improvement.

It was a new experience for me to participate as a candidate in an interview process that included three stages. It began with the standard interview with a committee consisting of school staff, board members, parents, and representatives from the community and district level. Then we proceeded to more rigorous stages. As candidates were whittled down to the committee's three top choices, those three participated in a process where the level of scrutiny was raised in subsequent interviews. The questions were far more probing and substantive. In the end, I found opportunities to engage in real discussions with each school's entire staff, followed by a session with parents and representatives from the community. It was the most holistic and rigorous interview process I had ever experienced. All committees participated in the final selection of their most preferred candidate. If ever there was an opportunity to reverse the erosion of trust in our public education system, the replication of the interview model described could restore that trust.

Disconnect Between Policymakers and Classroom Realities

Education happens in the classroom, and at its core it's the product of interactions between teachers and students. In an ideal world, those who are the most qualified in the field of education would manage our national education system at the highest level—and in every level in between—down to the classroom, where teachers do the day-to-day work of educating our students. But today's system is not ideal, and much of the difficulty comes from a disconnect between federal, state, and district policymakers and the realities teachers and students face together in the classroom.

The problems at the root of our education system seem at times like a bit of the "chicken and egg" conundrum. Which came first—poor leadership or the disconnect between decision makers and classroom realities? Because we've already reviewed some of the damage poor leadership does at the school level, we'll now explore the problem behind so many faulty schemes in our schools: policies that are driven by politics, bias, and a lack of understanding.

One overarching factor that impacts performance outcomes in classrooms across our entire education system is that policy decisions are passed down from federal, state, and district officials. Some in these highly consequential leadership positions do not have the qualifications or in-school experience to understand classroom dynamics or educational best practices. Too often, chasms are created when unqualified leaders mandate ill-advised policies without inquiring what resources will be needed to achieve those expectations. In other words, it's common for plans to be poorly developed and inadequately funded. The aerial view from the federal government level is different from the actual view of those most knowledgeable about the resources that are really needed—those who work so tirelessly at the ground level.

Instead of elevating the experience and insights of the staff who are doing the actual work of teaching students, the current system simply charges lower-level personnel with the responsibility of meeting mandated expectations. This is a problem in itself, but schools' ability to meet those expectations must also be put into context. Just as every classroom is a *micro* culture operating within the larger *macro* culture of an entire school, each school has a status within a school district, and each district has a status within a state. Schools that are located in lower-income communities consistently receive less funding and have facilities that are not properly equipped. Because their baseline resources are inadequate, they are already set up to fail.

So often, the obstacles federal, state, and local officials impose on school district leaders trickle down into classrooms. The obstacles include, but are not limited to, the fact that funds are attached to bureaucratic strings filled with unreasonable expectations—which often have nothing to do with improving the quality of education for students. Financial resources always come with required mandates wrapped into every bureaucratic dollar. While districts are constrained by a bureaucratic process requiring allocated funds to be spent how the federal and state education decision makers intend, basic needs go unfunded. To supersede outdated district priorities, it often takes a call to action from local advocates who recognize the urgency for change and support at the grassroots level. Unfortunately, the hard-earned experience and insights of qualified school leaders and teachers is left out of the equation when policies and budgets are set. Too often, ground-level educators are simply not given a space at the table where important decisions are made.

Furthermore, schools and districts are rarely, if ever, permitted to accurately report back to those in charge of allocating funds and provide feedback on why their mandates often miss their mark. Whatever the federal or state government's intended target or objective, the consequence of funds not achieving their desired outcome is that schools are stuck with trying to retrofit funded policies on top of ineffectual past and current policies, which further prevents any chance of cultivating exceptional classrooms.

When decision makers are out of sync with educational best practices and classroom realities, it can also strain internal school leadership. For instance, leaders of underfunded schools may use designated funds for critical needs rather than as the funds were intended to be used. In other circumstances where school leaders work with a school board or independent governing body, budgetary decisions are made collaboratively by a group. In preparing seasonal budgets, it is helpful for board members to meet regularly to routinely discuss the needs of the school. Generally, the more informed that board or PTA members are about the needs of the school, the better all participants are equipped to understand the proposed spending priorities. Oversight of a school's spending process at the school level has many advantages, versus the amount of funds allocated being determined by central-office employees who are familiar with finances but not schools. For example, during the fall, a school may initially intend to order a specific number of laptops during the upcoming budget cycle at the start of a new year for the following school year. But circumstances that occur during the school year make it necessary to reallocate funds intended for purchasing laptops toward the persistent shortage of curriculum resources repeatedly promised to teachers who have had to make do with outdated curriculum materials. In schools where boards are granted the autonomy to make budgeting decisions based on the needs of the school, requests for reallocation of funds are included on meeting agendas; and most of the time the board has the authority to arrive at a practical solution. This process works when teachers are included as members of the board and are given an opportunity to make it clear why the board is being asked to consider the proposed changes to the budget.

Unfortunately, those same independent parameters do not exist for most public schools in urban and rural communities. It can be an enormous burden at times to make spending decisions that are diametrically opposed to how state and local districts leaders specified funds were to be used, and then verify those decisions through an annual accounting report. It would not have to be a burden if a contingencies plan were in place that enabled schools to explain reasons for having to repurpose funding decisions and allowed the schools to submit receipts proving where the money was spent.

Here's an example. If the heating system inside of a school breaks down in the middle of winter and a request for immediate repairs is submitted through the bureaucratic pipeline, where emergency does not equate to urgency—as in it's mid-February with subfreezing temperatures—the school's ticket is on pause; because, like all things, the school must wait its turn for its request ticket to be honored. Distress messages are sent to implore department leaders in facilities about the dire conditions, yet five days later students and staff members are still expected to endure frigid temperatures. But by the third day, when there is no sign of the calvary arriving to address what is quickly escalating into a heath emergency, the school leader takes it upon him or herself to purchase space heaters for every classroom. Gym classes and the cafeteria get closed down due to the insufficient number of space heaters.

Schedules have been changed, and so have the minds of many students and staff, who no longer want to endure the freezing conditions and decide not to show up. Wearing winter coats but no hats or gloves, because families could not afford things deemed as accessories, made the conditions unbearable. Absences for students are recorded in the books; and when the school leader pleads with the enrollment and attendance department to allow him or her to forgive absences on the days the school was without adequate heat but is emphatically told "No"—well, we are witnessing the falling of one domino after another.

By the way, for members of the facilities department, who truly do care about the conditions inside of schools, prioritizing requests is a twofold challenge. In poor school districts, departments are also hit with significant budget cuts, which inevitably results in downsizing the number of employees. So in addition to a smaller work staff, almost every other request for services has been waiting in an inbox on a desk that was recently occupied by someone who managed the flow of requests, but they were among the employees let go. So broken toilets in the bathroom of one school result in the custodian's turning off the water. A broken sink that eventually fell to the floor was taken care of by shutting off the valve to stop the flow of water. The new sink is stored in the custodian's crowded office until someone can install it. When that will happen seems unclear, but those of us familiar with the terrain of schools at the ground level are guessing it could take weeks.

Then we wonder how schools manage to survive on budgets too small to cover the big catastrophes that occur at the ground level. Because there are no contingency forms allowing some school leaders to explain the circumstances for diverting funds elsewhere, they are sometimes caught between an unethical rock and an unethical hard place. Resorting to submitting false data in order to remain in compliance or retain the good graces of organization leaders at the district and state level is a real conundrum.

Over the course of my 15-year leadership tenure, I found it totally unacceptable for students to arrive at school in the middle of winter wearing a sweater or spring jacket and no gloves or boots. The majority of those students lived in foster homes, youth shelters, or Transitional Living Programs. Unable to request funds from the school's budget, I, like so many teachers, used my personal funds to make sure students were adequately clothed during harsh weather conditions. A staff member and I would take the students to one of those big box stores and let them select a new winter coat, accessories, and, when needed, a pair of boots. Like so many adults in schools located in poor communities across the country, in moments like those I would have preferred to have access to a school emergency fund. Instead we are subjected to policies reflecting a total lack of awareness of the realistic conditions occurring at the school level. Policymakers responsible for budget decisions create untenable situations for all school staff in certain zip codes, which further erodes morale and confidence.

It complicates matters even further when districts and schools have to describe, in detail, the direct impact allotted funds had on performance outcomes. Talk about being caught between a rock and a hard place! In some districts, schools teetering on threats of closure or receivership file overly positive reports rather than responding truthfully and ethically. They feel compelled to appease those in charge of the purse strings or those who occupy positions of political influence.

These school leaders recognize that remaining open in communities of great need is paramount. So, they give in to the bias-based performative scheme and submit reports containing slight or blatant exaggerations in order to appear in compliance with funds tied to expectations. It's a vicious cycle wherein school leaders find ways to escape the immense pressure on their school's survival—but at the cost of their honesty and professional integrity. District and government policies created without input from school leaders are another reason for gaps in instruction, morale, and trust in bureaucrats, who rarely make in-person visits to schools—particularly underperforming schools impacted by their budget decisions.

Meanwhile, underfunded schools are forced to consider tactics that slightly misrepresent facts to stay afloat so they can remain open for another school year. The gravest harm in opting to fudge reports is that, when outcomes are reported as factually correct but are not, it perpetuates the cycle of being dismissive of facts. It also greatly diminishes trust in our educational system. And it can provide false evidence for poorly designed "improvements." Being beholden to standards of *appearances* instead of factual and measurable data intended to be true indicators of performance outcomes linked with academic standards is a self-perpetuating failure. When educators lack efficacy in reporting truthful and accurate performance outcomes, it compromises our ability to trust reports. If Efficacy Report Cards were required of every state, how many would earn a failing grade?

How Social Stigmas Influence School Budgets

Historically, school districts throughout our nation's poor communities have been deprived of adequate funding resources. The justification for withholding financial and other educational resources that could have given all children equal access to a quality education was the belief that it was not necessary to invest in quality education in communities populated with people of color and thought to be intellectually inferior.

The perpetual cycle of underfunding those schools is one of the factors contributing to substandard education today. Continuing the pattern of underfunding schools inevitably created and maintained low academic performance expectations. Failing performance outcomes were fueled by substandard education practices in poorly funded schools. The predictable cycle of poor educational outcomes conveniently fueled the stereotypical but false assertion that students were intellectually inferior—until education reforms initiatives proved that assertion to be incorrect. Several college and university education programs researched and discovered barriers that caused inequities. When higher education institutions launched partnerships with schools in low-income neighborhoods to minimize, and where possible eradicate, those barriers, in many cases the newly introduced educational models upended and disproved the myths of intellectual inferiority.

The Failure to Replicate Promising Education Reforms

Many reform efforts were able to prove a direct correlation between access to quality models of education and the real intellectual ability of children and youth living in poor communities. The era of education reforms seemed so promising. Unfortunately, several initiatives worthy of grant expansions encountered hard deadlines from various donors, or school administrators were unable to convince others to continue making contributions. Unless districts are willing to absorb the cost of continuing reform initiatives, most do not continue beyond the date of expiration. Many schools are unable to continue with reforms because the small budget they were allocated was not only insufficient but the reason they partnered in the first place with outside grant-funded programs to address some of the education resource gaps. Despite many leaders of education reforms being aware of the need to work with schools to codify initiatives that showed improved performance outcomes, they were constricted by either time or insufficient means to refund programs. Codification is a process required to transition reforms into teaching practices as a means of making changes permanent and sustainable prior to the expiration of grants.

Another measure considered was finding a means to replicate new, credible best practices across several schools or throughout entire districts. More often than not, when the first or additional number of grant-funded cycles eventually came to an end, schools felt the immediate impact of the absence of their short-lived, highly valued resources. Many of the grants for programs included salaries for additional staffing positions to lead the new programs. Some reform initiatives required additional staff to administer and monitor programs to ensure adherence to grant guidelines and specifications, one of the criteria for reapplying for grant renewals. Another critical criterion for determining reapplication eligibility status was data. Grant funders relied on data to justify decisions to extend or terminate partnerships.

Despite a number of education reforms successfully disproving the intellectual-inferiority lie, external funding sources that came to an end proved how over-reliance on funding sources beyond school budgets could negatively impact gains made. Especially devastated were inner city schools that had no capacity to retain the level of staffing needed to maintain fully operational programs created under education reforms. To be clear, not all educational reforms produced successful outcomes. However, it was an era that ushered in our country's greatest potential of proving how improvements to our education system could net higher student performance outcomes, just by providing them equitable access to quality educational resources.

Education Reform Pioneers Who Succeeded

African American educational pioneers like Marva Collins and Geoffrey Canada are among a group of prolific innovators invested in advancing academic achievement in predominantly Black communities. Marva Collins was a teacher in the Chicago Public Schools. She was so dissatisfied with the poor educational standards that in 1975 she decided to start her own school, Westside Preparatory School. Marva was driven by the belief that elevating learning expectations of students could be achieved through a more rigorous education experience. She proved that teaching up to each student's true level of intellectual capability, by setting educational standards high and providing rigorous instruction, was essential to each student's educational prosperity (TheHistoryMakers.org/biography/marva-collins-40).

Geoffrey Canada has been and continues to be devoted to meeting the needs of children and families through a unique program, the Harlem Children's Zone (HCZ). The HCZ attended to the educational needs of students in the Promise Academy Charter Schools. But valuing the awareness of an entire community's well-being, Geoffrey viewed his role as an education reformer through a humanitarian lens that saw beyond the needs of children inside of schools. Fully aware of the challenging conditions generated by poverty, which has a way of gripping whole communities, the HCZ designed a community-based resource model to circumvent the current constraints of inadequate resources needed to address the health and wellness of children and their families. Geoffrey boldly decided to target the root causes serving as barriers to each citizen's right to live in vibrant communities, by dedicating resources to nurture entire families. The addition of community centers and other facilities created spaces for outreach services, informing citizens about government support programs, filing taxes, and developing healthy lives through eating well and exercising. The vision was for the Harlem Children's Zone to embody the broader needs and aspirations of whole communities.

The Promise Academy Charter Schools were essential hubs of Geoffrey's social experiment. But to ensure academic success in the Academies, Geoffrey and his team knew the importance of preparing babies and preschoolers for future success in their elementary through college years. The addition of Baby College for zero- to three-year-olds, of Three Year Old Journey Programs, and of Harlem Gems three-to-five-year-old programs represented Geoffrey's extraordinary vision. He was someone totally devoted to creating the conditions for academic success inside of schools by seeing them as an extension of whole communities in need of reforms. Decades later, evidence of the model's success can be seen in the performance outcomes of students who routinely perform at the level of valedictorians and then go on to successfully complete college-degree programs. Over the span of 30-plus years, the Harlem Children's Zone and education programs have been models of success, producing highly educated graduates poised for future success in higher education and careers. Geoffrey Canada's innovative and visionary leadership is an example of highly successful educational models worthy of being replicated. Readers interested in learning more can find additional information at HCZ.org, *Community Members Matter/Harlem Children's Zone*.

Innovative educators such as Marva Collins and Geoffrey Canada launched new schools driven by an ideology that redefined *quality education* in America. Under their individual leadership, their education programs successfully led to school cultures that changed the trajectory of education outcomes, transforming students who were likely previously marked to achieve marginal success at best into scholars who habitually performed at the highest academic levels.

Instead of focusing on debunking the myth of intellectual inferiority, Marva, Geoffrey, and other innovative thinkers devoted their time identifying a better quality of educational resources. Changes to methods of instruction enhanced teaching practices. Teaching practices paired with high expectations, made clear to all students, were essential to inspiring students with the belief they possessed the ability to learn. Higher performance outcomes were an indication of each student's true intellectual learning capacity. It is of immeasurable value to surround students with caring, compassionate educators unwilling to waver in their convictions that high academic achievement is possible. What may have been perceived as impossible by others was unacceptable to the Marva Collinses and Geoffrey Canadas. Their persistence in the belief of what students are truly capable of achieving inspired their determination to prove high academic achievements are attainable among all children—regardless of race, ethnicity, or socio-economic status. Why is it monumentally important to discover how we can influence the trajectory of each student's educational journey by simply tailoring our expectations? Because our level of expectation influences every other decision, including quality of curriculum selected, how lessons are designed, and degree of rigor embedded in instruction. The degree to which students are academically challenged is what elevates learning. Fundamentally, it comes down to what we believe students are capable of achieving, and then instilling those beliefs in the students. Thankfully, Marva and Geoffrey gave students confidence in their ability to be academic scholars accustomed to success. Students' aspirations soared. So did the rate of students accepted to college to earn four-year college degrees. When educational glass ceilings are removed, access to future career opportunities with higher income potential is the prosperity we should want for all students.

Communities that do not have the benefit of innovative pioneers have so few options; and even lesser chances of partaking in inspirationally led educational experiences. We've seen how federal and state policymakers fail to support schools by pushing untested changes and not giving school leaders and staff the opportunity to bring their hard-earned wisdom to the table. These are critical issues, and they are accompanied by another pervasive problem: schools are not funded at levels that enable them to meet the education needs of each student. At the highest levels of government, an equitable education for every student must be a priority. Policymakers and stakeholders must be invested in the value of a quality education for every American child—and allocate the funds needed to provide that education.

At the ground level, one of the key roles of school administrators is to support teachers and classrooms. How well they fulfill that role varies from school to school. In part, it depends on the abilities of the school leaders, as well as the resources the school has access to. Even in the best scenarios, a great deal of school administrators' leadership time is consumed by the need to respond to the bureaucratic demands of their district's and state's department of education. Instead of being able to focus on supporting their teachers and students, administrators' attention is divided. Too often, instead of receiving support from district-level officials, they find their concerns dismissed.

It's not uncommon for school leaders' requests for professional resources and training to be ignored by upper-level officials for years, until a newsworthy incident occurs and officials assemble a rapid-response team—to do what? Option A: they douse the embarrassing firestorm created by the media in the hopes it will quickly go away and avoid further public scrutiny. Or Option B: they inquire at the school level about what resources are needed to genuinely resolve the problem.

If school-level staff are never allowed a seat at meetings where pivotal decisions are made, Option A is almost always the default response. Then everyone can quickly pivot back to the normal routines of attending to expectations related to the usual bureaucratic consumption of educational time. Expectations generated at the highest levels generally come with the need for school leaders to devote time placating those in charge of creating useless and time-consuming mandates at the executive or district level. Neither does much to promote or elevate learning in classrooms.

CHAPTER 2

Symptoms

JUST AS WE REVIEWED THE CORE PROBLEMS HAMPERING OUR national education system, it's important to understand the varied ways these problems surface in classrooms and schools across the country. In general, these issues can be viewed as either facility centered or staff centered.

Run-Down Schools

The absolute worst combination of worrisome issues for any school is a pervasive lack of high-level leadership, inadequate budgets, and schools that are not physically equipped to be places of learning. In many underperforming public schools where underfunded budgets are standard practice, students are being educated in some of the most deplorable conditions. It is unreasonable to expect students to focus on learning inside of dilapidated buildings with worn-out plumbing, inadequate electrical systems, lack of ventilation, or broken heating/cooling units. Classrooms and common areas, like gymnasiums and cafeterias, become inaccessible due to poor plumbing or heating conditions. Finding alternative space to accommodate students reassigned to available classrooms imposes greater responsibility on new and veteran teachers assigned larger numbers of students than what is generally deemed permissible. This overwhelms all teachers, but especially new ones.

Everyone—from school principals to teachers to support staff (if they even exist) to students and their families—is contending with extraordinary circumstances due to generations of extreme neglect, which makes those public schools feel more like places where students are being warehoused rather than educated.

In those schools, such disruption is unwelcomed and unwanted, but everyone is forced to tolerate it. While the degree of despair in many poorly functioning schools is not an exaggeration, in fairness to many urban public schools, the conditions are not always the same; there are a number of well-managed and successful schools even in poor neighborhoods. Unfortunately, those schools are often tethered to unfair stereotypes, so it's assumed that because of where they are located, they too are classified as dysfunctional and unsafe.

Competent and skilled school leaders and staff try to make do with the scarcity of adequate resources their schools receive—and the meager attention and assistance they receive from district leaders. Still, no amount of exaggeration could adequately portray the impact of outdated, unsanitary, and unsafe environments that make learning all but impossible to achieve. As cringeworthy as it all sounds, we cannot fix problems without being willing to shine a spotlight on the plight of staff members and students trying to function under the most deplorable conditions.

School Staff in Crisis

Inadequate support for teachers and school staff is one of the primary conditions that negatively impact our ability to cultivate exceptional classrooms. Examining this problem and providing a plan to fix it is a core goal of this book because it is only by giving teachers the support they need and deserve that we can reliably and measurably improve educational outcomes for every student, regardless of where they live.

As we consider the circumstances facing school staff today, we see three areas that are most critical and in need of change: the plight of first-year teachers, the untenable combination of extreme understaffing and overcrowding, and the cost of a loss of trust.

The Precarious Position of First-Year Teachers

Some districts—especially those without adequate resources—assign new teachers the same volume of responsibilities as their more seasoned colleagues. Expecting new teachers to produce immediate and sustainable positive results is unfair, regardless of whether they were hired in a well-funded or poorly funded school district. But most well-funded school districts do not set up first-year teachers to fail. (This is one reason for the higher rate of candidates applying for teaching positions in affluent school districts.)

New teachers in well-run schools can rely on their leadership team as their absolute "go to" people when they need a safety net or guidance, and this leadership support is a critical part of retaining good teachers. In this way, districts that provide more than peer mentoring throughout the first year of new teacher's tenure are taking responsibility for nurturing the progress of inexperienced teachers. Because staff work with new teachers to advance their continued progression along their professional learning curve, schools in these districts have a higher retention rate. New teachers in school districts that provide a range of professional development resources progress much more quickly than those who must rely on their own resilience and instincts, and students are the beneficiaries.

But in many other schools, new teachers are largely left on their own. These very teachers are likely among those who have already decided to leave their new position or are currently contemplating an early departure. Schools that are preoccupied with a need to invest in survival tactics, like reassigning students to already overpopulated classrooms due to staffing shortages, hinder opportunities to create a culture that enables teachers to thrive professionally. This has a direct bearing on student outcomes because every teacher's ability to excel as an educator is an essential link to ensure that "thriving" traits are passed along to students. Teachers must receive quality resources and support in order to provide quality education.

One of the most egregious misconceptions rarely recognized by school districts is their assumption that new teachers are fully capable of taking on all of the same challenging and broad responsibilities of a seasoned veteran teacher on day one. They are not.

First-year teachers are offered positions based on the favorable impression they made on interview committee members. Committee members asked questions, listened to each candidate's responses, observed the candidates' overall demeanor, and considered other factors to determine who among those being interviewed did or said something to demonstrate they would be the best complementary fit with their school's culture. Sometimes those who showed the most promise have a short-lived tenure. Much to the selection committee's surprise, many new teachers make unforeseen early departures, sometimes within the first few months of their first year.

The daily responsibilities of a teacher's life are multifaceted, highly demanding, and challenging. The expectation that new teachers are well prepared to take on the broad range of responsibilities necessary for educating students is unfair and sets up both teachers and students for failure. Since the majority of first-year teachers do not possess teaching experience beyond a one-year internship, a single year of training is insufficient preparation for them to independently take on the enormous range of responsibilities.

Symptoms

In every industry, organization, or profession, newly hired employees are entitled to be novices. Like every newly hired employee, first-year teachers who are hired based on their promising potential need time and resources to help them evolve from novice to competent educators. Each of the various responsibilities in the teaching profession is highly complex. Not all districts recognize that new teachers lack an awareness of and adequate preparation for taking on the complexities of managing a class. But promising novice teachers need access to professional development resources to help them grow and progress along their professional learning curve.

The laborious process of organizing and managing classrooms is usually beyond the scope of what new teachers were expecting—if they arrived anticipating they would have the luxury of focusing solely on what they were trained to teach and what was verified in the job description. Newly hired teachers' euphoria tends to dissipate upon discovering that the position described in writing is far different from the one they happily accepted. If prospective candidates were fully informed during interviews about the true size and scope of responsibilities involved in teaching, one cannot help wondering if most would decline the position.

And yet each year this population of enthusiastic novices arrive to their first day of school full of expectations and aspirations of becoming a competent teacher. But if they lack experience handling disruptive students who, in the early days of school, constantly defy the teacher's authority, which prevents other students from engaging in lessons, those aspirations are quickly replaced with a feeling of inadequacy. First-year teachers who devote an enormous amount of time and energy addressing petulant misbehaving students—and have little to no success—are right to question whether or not they chose the proper profession. It is common for new teachers to feel vulnerable if they are just thrown into classrooms without lifejackets and expected to sink or swim. To avoid drowning, their decision to quit may feel like the only alternative available when school administrators—who also were denied access to professional development resources that would equip them with strategies for successful intervention—meet repeated requests for assistance with tepid responses.

Imagine what it must be like for eager teachers who arrive at their first day of school harboring high of hopes for a great school year, only to discover that having the best of intentions simply was not enough. Within a number of days or the first few weeks, most new teachers gradually realize that they are inadequately prepared for the situation they are confronted with. They are inadequately prepared to respond to incidents that start small but quickly grow beyond anything they were trained to address—or ever imagined.

How Systemically Failing School Culture Impedes Teachers' Success

In the aftermath of situations where teachers had to repeatedly call upon the school administration cavalry to put out yet another fire that ended in students' being assigned elsewhere in the building or being suspended, they realize that the cavalry has a default response for addressing almost every disruptive student: just remove them. At some point, the bigger picture starts to come into focus for many new teachers: they recognize that the conditions of the class they inherited mirror the level of disruptive conduct permitted throughout the school, and both problems seem too insurmountable to overcome. While it's tempting to suggest that these conditions are found primarily in underfunded schools in urban communities, furthering this stereotypical narrative is unproductive. In addition, recent events make it pretty clear that incidents of disruptive behaviors are steadily increasing in communities that once never imagined being visited by mass shootings or having to endure lockdowns in their school district. Systemic failures aren't restricted to geographical borders or community income levels.

When any new teacher—in any school, in any community—finds their professional experiences so intolerable, they do what others do in turbulent circumstances that seem to have no end in sight: they quit. They were not told to expect and be prepared for turbulence in the classroom. They were not equipped to teach effectively in our current impaired school system.

These challenges affect schools in a range of communities, but schools in lower-income areas are often targeted with a disproportionate amount of negative public commentary. However, it's seldom acknowledged that much of the current turbulence results from economic and social barriers erected centuries ago to stave off any attempts to interrupt or weaken the status quo. News reports of violence in urban schools or surrounding neighborhoods fuel outcries demanding the closure of "those" urban schools, which always underperform while being mired in rampant lawless behaviors. How unfortunate that—rather than finding ways to not blame the majority of residents, who truly do yearn to live in safe communities, or punish students attending historically underfunded schools—critics prefer to gaslight and use negative narratives about failing schools in poor communities to their advantage.

A commonly used scenario by those invested in "making a case for promoting school closure" generally begins with embedding fear in one population at the expense of another population. The goal is to support efforts to get and maintain the public's attention on scary incidents that, over time, are meant to emerge into a pattern or cycle of similar incidents. Fomenting fear is how you generate justification for others who are easily convinced just by the mere suggestion of something being a bigger and more worrisome concern than it actually is. Media outlets are usually a reliable source for routinely reporting incidents of violence, regardless if incidents involve only a few students in schools or youths in communities. The media conveniently omits the fact that incidents in poor communities may be traced to inadequate safety, less access to counseling, and less access to other useful measures—whereas all of these benefits tend to be available to citizens living in affluent communities. But the point isn't to put out fires, it's using incidents to inflame others and persuade people residing outside of those communities that things are way out of control. We've become accustomed to cultivating fear, which is such a useful tool for exacerbating situations. Rather than devoting time to explore the root causes and committing the right kind of resources to resolve issues, the knee-jerk response is to buy into a narrative that instills fear, which overrides our ability to use common sense.

Lacking supportive intervention strategies to address and tamp-down incidents at the onset, new and veteran teachers are left feeling helpless. Over time, if there is a continual absence of support and teachers experience more failure in their attempts to hold disruptive students accountable, self-confidence gradually erodes. Predictably, if no meaningful intervention is made available, the continued erosion of a teacher's self-confidence produces a sense of fragility. Aspirations of becoming a successful teacher are replaced with preoccupations of their inability to manage their classroom. Being left to handle matters themselves understandably makes them pause, examine the situation, and conclude with a self-assessment of whether or not they possess the necessary qualifications to meet expectations. Like their students who experience disappointment after repeated failures, if there is no meaningful source of intervention to reverse course, teachers fall into various stages of learned helplessness.

Despondency is a commonly shared experience of students and teachers in underfunded schools that perpetually ignore the needs of those who value but cannot gain access to quality education. Fear of failure is being cultivated across a variety of places in our education system. It is due in part to our being conditioned to accept the current substandard conditions rather than emphatically declaring, "This is totally unacceptable!" But just declaring it is unacceptable is not enough. We must make such declarations represent actionable steps we are prepared to take, including, when needed, throwing down the proverbial gauntlet or drawing definitive lines in the sand indicating how much we mean it. It takes a willingness to identify steps and then begin the process of actually shifting in a new direction where, instead of being bystanders, we accept the responsibility of being agents of change. Eradication of problems contributing to the ongoing exodus of teachers in public schools requires a truthful examination of root causes. Here's an example of how we can support and keep new teachers.

Working Toward a Solution

First, districts and schools must make retaining new teachers a top priority. But declarations of making new teachers a "top priority" alone will not retain new teachers. Declarations, coupled with resources that will ensure their professional growth, are absolutely necessary. Students are assigned to classes where subjects are taught over the course of an entire school year. The assumption is having a year to learn Algebra or other subjects will provide enough time for students to potentially achieve mastery in the subject. If we view and value the professional growth cycle of new teachers, a timeline for learning and growing proficiency in the acquisition of new skills is similar to the stages of learning that students go through. Both need to be viewed through the lens of a yearlong process. In fact, districts and schools can start by mapping out a yearlong professional development plan to teach inexperienced first-year teachers about best practices. The learning of best practices will need to be routinely revisited, and time must be allowed for new teachers to develop their comfort zone with using the practices they've learned. Time to learn and apply what is learned happens by providing new teachers with ongoing training and consulting throughout the school year to ensure their professional growth. We have seen enough evidence of what happens when new teachers are expected to independently progress from novice to competent educators without professional development resources. It's time to break the cycle of expecting proficient performance from first-year teaching novices.

We know that in every profession first-year employees need access to mentoring and guidance by experienced professionals in order to advance their progress along their learning curve. It simply is not enough to rely on a candidate's promising potential. Possessing potential is no real indicator that teachers will arrive with the level of knowledge and tools to self-supervise their own growth. Like newbies in any profession, first-year teachers are poised and eager to achieve, or even surpass, the interview committee's initial expectations—if their professional development needs are not neglected. Early departures from the teaching profession are so often linked to red flags that are frequently unseen or selectively ignored.

When a new teacher's requests for help go unheard or unseen, it unleashes fissures in the teacher's confidence and erodes their confidence in school leadership and peers. Recall what occurs when aspirations are replaced with self-doubt and eventually professional fragility. When fragility overcomes self-confidence and aspirations that were so enthusiastically shared during interviews, the anticipated joy of joining the teaching profession fades from memory, and teachers instead become preoccupied with thoughts of how to survive from one day to the next.

Interview-committee members, and ultimately school leaders, must not only welcome and congratulate candidates but also provide professional development resources supported by in-school training sessions so the promising potential that first-year teachers displayed during interviews will have an opportunity to flourish. The handshake ritual congratulating chosen candidates must include time to review a list of district and school resources available to assist their professional growth. If you have ever served on an interview committee, you may recall the eagerness of candidates who made their desire to pursue a long-term career in education so clear during their interview. It is incumbent on committee members and school administrators to repay the chosen candidate's promise to educate all children to the best of their ability with tools and resources that will enable them to achieve their promise.

Attending to their professional needs is how school districts retain new teachers. Hiring new teachers is the first goal in the hiring process. Retention of new teachers must be the second overarching goal. Retention is possible through the availability of meaningful resources linked with real experiences they will encounter in classrooms. Teachers want their work and efforts valued. Support tailored to respond to conditions inside of classrooms is how district and school leaders show new teachers their efforts and work are valued. It will also enable them to bring their teaching aspirations to fruition.

Currently, some school districts assign veteran teachers to mentor to new teachers, but veteran teachers still have the responsibilities of teaching their own classes and are typically overextended already. Furthermore, they are not provided with professional resources to pass along to their mentees. Ideally, a mentor's role should be to help new teachers access the safety nets and professional resources that each school already has in place. But the current resources mentors inform new teachers about generally relate to school supply closets, where the custodian's office is, and helping them become familiar with school policies. The real lifejackets that are needed to lengthen the life expectancy of a new teacher's career do not yet exist.

In Part 2 we will look more closely at the professional resources, in the form of professional development specialists who should be available to consult, train, and guide new teachers. Having these resources present in schools would enable each teacher to progress their competency and overall professional growth in all areas needed to cultivate exceptional classrooms. Additional upsides to adding the resources of professional development specialists is keeping schools fully staffed and improving student performance.

Chronic Understaffing and Overcrowding: An Untenable Situation

One of the most frequently cited reasons for the increased exodus from the teaching profession is the challenge of managing disruptive behaviors in classrooms. Or to be more accurate, it is really the absence of adequate professional development training for managing disruptive behaviors in any classroom. Overpopulated classrooms exacerbate any teacher's ability to manage disruptive behaviors. But for new teachers, who are the least experienced with managing a student population of any size, it is probably a disaster in the making. The pattern of schools losing, then substituting, and eventually replacing new teachers is in full effect for one reason: our public education system neglects the needs of first-year teachers.

Of course, this ongoing drain affects veteran teachers as well, and the result is an environment where abrupt departures are now becoming the norm. By mid-year the annual ritual begins: administrators scramble to find substitutes to replace new teachers. Many substitute teachers are licensed but never met qualifications for full-time teaching positions. Then, predictably, untrained substitutes are unlikely to remain. Their departure creates a revolving-door effect—the perpetual need to cycle in new replacements to replace the previous replacements. As stressful as it is for school leaders and teachers, this wasteful process inevitably negatively impacts students the most. And when combined with the budgetary pressure to keep staffing at a minimum, both teachers and students are set up to fail.

In recent years, schools have undergone numerous changes that make conditions less than ideal for instruction and learning in traditional spaces. Overcrowded classrooms are currently one of the major impediments in advancing students' education. A teacher's ability to teach is hindered when overflowing populations of students are assigned to classes. In the effort to just manage large populations of students, many teachers turn to activities that are intended to keep students occupied until the bell rings, signaling it's time to move on to the next class. Most common among those measures is assigning students busywork or turning a math class into a study period. How else can a teacher originally assigned a population of 20 students be expected to manage and teach 35, 40, or more? And what if many of the excess students are not scheduled to be in a math period, yet they are assigned to spaces based on the criterion of seat availability? Whether or not the subject being taught is aligned with their schedule, many students assigned to seats based on availability are actually in classrooms filled beyond maximum capacity. Those not assigned to the math class still must attend. It does raise the question: Why are students randomly assigned to classes not on their schedule expected to forfeit their right to an education?

Overcrowded classrooms and decreasing numbers of staff members are the result of severe budget cuts, as are the unsafe and deteriorating conditions inside of old buildings. And yet, any expectation of cultivating exceptional classrooms starts with an assumption that none of those problems exist. As we examine the problems that plague our schools, we must remember not to fixate on the symptoms, but to focus on, and determine to eliminate, the root causes of those symptoms.

So, while reading this book, take some time to visit your neighborhood school or reach out to school staff to assess the current conditions of classrooms. Transparent assessments of classroom conditions should be verified. If, while walking through a school, you come upon classrooms containing desks stacked so tightly together it restricts the movement of students squeezed into spaces that prevent even minimal efforts to physically navigate from their desk to other locations inside of their classrooms, it's overcrowded. Under such circumstances, lack of mobility creates constraints for non-disabled students. One cannot help but wonder how disabled students negotiate their way in and around overcrowded classrooms.

Overflowing numbers of students assigned to spaces designed to seat smaller populations is problematic from a logistics standpoint alone. However, another serious problem with overcrowded conditions is that they are often in violation of federal and state safety regulations. Annual fire inspections are carried out to ensure everyone's safety and make sure all school facilities meet fire and safety codes. But concerned parents and teachers must ask: If the number of students assigned each class exceeds the number deemed acceptable and safe, how do schools manage to pass their annual fire inspection?

While each of the preceding areas of concern ought to be worrisome, overcrowded classrooms are also not conducive to providing quality instruction or learning. Several education organizations, including the National Education Association (NEA), have reported similar findings. As recently as 2019 in an *NEA News* article, "Educators and Parents Reset the Class Size Debate," author Tim Walker concluded, "Overcrowded classrooms populated by large numbers of students is detrimental to learning." NEA makes clear "the ideal classroom size is fifteen students." (nea.org NEA News, NEA Today article *Educators and Parents Reset the Class Size Debate*, Tim Walker 2.8.2019).

In the same article, Rutgers University professor Bruce Baker echoed the need for small classes, stating, "Ample research indicates that children in smaller classes achieve better outcomes, both academic and otherwise, and that class size reduction can be an effective strategy for closing racial and socioeconomic achievement gaps."

Within a 2019 policy brief was a chart titled "Benefit of Small Class Size," in which the NEA showed numerous benefits of small class size.

Among them were early identification of learning disabilities, improved high school graduation rates, and large reduction in discipline referrals ("Class Size Reduction: A Proven Reform Strategy," nea.org, 2019). The findings in the policy were reinforced by Baker, California, teachers, parents, and others cited in the article, all of whom were advocating for smaller class size. Overall, smaller class sizes have been found to make it possible for teachers to spend more time focused on instruction, which is the intended mission of our education system. Overcrowded classrooms produce overwrought teachers forced to exchange schoolbooks for discipline manuals outlining their school policies and procedures for managing disruptive behaviors. Honestly, when conditions become a combination of bedlam and babysitting services due to overflowing student populations, with no end in sight, it makes exit doors for teachers that much easier to find.

As explained in the *NEA Today* article, "Educators and Parents Reset the Class Size Debate," reducing class size is complicated. Historically, the issue has resurfaced during times of recessions and during recoveries from recessions. Many teachers and school leaders endured the unpleasant crisis caused by the 2008 recession. School budgets shrank, which naturally precipitated the layoffs of numerous teachers and school staff. Those teachers who were fortunate enough to retain their positions became the collateral damage, along with students, when class sizes in many schools doubled and teachers were assigned additional overcrowded classes to cover. One has to ask: How much learning can occur under those conditions?

Recessions do serve as a reminder of how history has a way of repeating itself. Recovering from any recession tends to leave a lingering taste of mistrust. But the recovery from the 2008 recession never really occurred in many school districts. What was supposed to be a recovery instead became a way to permanently normalize the reduction of school budgets. The financial crisis was used to justify deeper cuts, but when the economy rebounded, most schools' budgets were never restored.

The post-2008 period revealed a major shift in education. Prior to the 2008 recession, budgets in school districts were already beginning to decline. Many educators expected that budget levels would at least return to the pre-recession levels of allocation, but that did not occur. Why? Because in America, once people get used to having to make do with less, while also being expected to produce at high standards, those in positions of power normalize austerity measures. Public schools in poor districts are constantly forced to adjust to smaller budgets. In this case, even when the government did replenish some of the funding during the recovery, not all schools received the allocation of funds needed to return their previous bare-bones budget back to bare-bones status. Schools that were underperforming prior to the recession were forced to invent ways to make do on more stringent resources after the recovery. Consequently, they inherited additional layers of substandard educational conditions that made it almost impossible to reverse the continued downward trajectory of academic performance outcomes of students enrolled in those schools. Simply put, education was not on the same level of priority as banks (who created the economic crisis and were rewarded with billions), and public schools that were never adequately funded were simply subjected to additional crises from which they would never be able to recover.

In every budget cycle, the allocation of funding sources mirrored the decline in school budgets, which foreshadowed the closing of more schools. Meanwhile, the federal government increased funding support to wealthy corporations that aspired to expand charter schools. In fact, few privately funded public independent and charter schools are concerned about overcrowded classrooms. Why? They know that if their programs are to succeed, the size of student populations in classrooms matters. Adequate funding is based on an understanding of how the size of populations directly influences every teacher's ability to teach and every student's ability to learn. Such impediments to instruction as overcrowding simply are not tolerated. Retaining teachers will require reconfiguring budgets to reduce student populations. Clearly, limited school budgets are among the root causes of overcrowded classrooms, and overcrowded classrooms provide the impetus for new teachers to leave the profession. And what happens when we fail to attract and retain new teachers?

Exodus of Experienced Leaders

The current rapid pace of filling teaching positions is borne out of the need to reassure the public that schools are either almost fully staffed or at full capacity. Masking the truth about staff departures is a short-lived ploy, particularly when parents and students arrive at school and discover the teachers they were expecting are no longer there. Districts' desperation to reassure parents and students—but mostly parents—that all is well and education will proceed as expected has caused some loosening of hiring standards. That should worry everyone.

But more worrisome is the instability caused by the recent uptick in departures by principals, school committee members, and superintendents. Among those leaving are some of the most highly qualified and dedicated leaders, who have proven track records of success over a span of years.

Though education has been an especially challenging career path for many years, the COVID pandemic has stripped the field of many of its best leaders and accelerated the unraveling of our school system. Despite their best efforts to tolerate the confusion that arose from constantly revising and defending health and safety protocols during COVID, many educators were worn down by the strain. For others with higher tolerance levels, the decision to remain meant having to steel themselves in ways they never previously imagined as leaders in education. School administrators endured unexpected, and in some cases highly disruptive, discord between members of their school community. In the midst of the panic caused by the pandemic and its impact on our economy, many community members became unwilling to address concerns in the usual way; in some communities, adherence to rules of cordiality to resolve disagreements all but disappeared. Former traditions of abiding by meeting protocols, where manners and respectful conduct were the norm, now seemed quaint and from an entirely different era.

Powerful alliances among school staff, principals, and school board and committee members were tested. Eventually public meetings became so unruly that cooperative alliances began to weaken. Many citizens' legitimate concerns were never heard because of the disruptions and heightened level of acrimony.

School leaders found themselves unprepared to manage the constant fluctuation of having to defend changing district policies while being opposed by teachers, staff members, and parents. Being quite familiar with staff members they had known and respected for many years, some school leaders knew that staff demands for absolute and non-negotiable proof of safety standards were not unreasonable.

In many cases, administrators were caught between district mandates and teachers who, fearing for the personal safety of students and themselves, fought to retain masking and social-distancing standards. Absent those minimum standards, school staff members were unwilling to risk their lives when remote learning was available as a safer option. While unable to openly acknowledge that their staff members' concerns echoed their own fears and concerns, school leaders knew they were in a lose-lose position.

The challenge for all school leaders, but particularly those who decided to quit, came down to myriad reasons: having to constantly juggle untested safety mandates over a three-year period; having to dodge threats of violence from people who vehemently opposed vaccines and wearing masks; and attempting to convince their staff and students' families that it was safe enough to return to school for in-person learning in the midst of increasing hospitalizations and deaths. These and many other difficulties served to compound one challenge after another in a growing list of other alarming concerns, until school leaders were at a breaking point.

For many educators, the conditions prior to COVID incited moments of wanting to retire earlier than originally planned. But the arrival of COVID brought more clarity about the unfairness of expectations placed on educators, which then widened the fissures that had been festering for quite some time in the teaching profession.

CHAPTER 3

How Problems Affect Students

SO FAR, WE'VE EXAMINED HOW FAILED LEADERSHIP AT THE highest levels, compounded by inadequate funding and the unprecedented challenges of the COVID-19 pandemic, has weakened our national education system and led to a diminished population of qualified educators. But students are the real victims of unexpected, abrupt departures, overcrowding, understaffing, and the many associated ills.

The Weight of Teacher Turnover

Adults are often impressed with how malleable and resilient most children are in the face of difficult circumstances, leaving us to marvel at their level of recovery. But we do them a disservice when we expect students to settle down and quickly recuperate in the aftermath of a teacher's unexpected exit. Typically, what occurs next is that the position is temporarily filled with a substitute teacher while the interview committee is quickly reassembled to restart the interview process in search of what they hope will be a permanent replacement.

If you have had the occasion to visit a school after one of those early departures, you might have detected something about the school community's equilibrium being a bit out of sorts. What is often overlooked is the level of anxiety students experience the day they learn about the teacher's decision to leave. The degree of uncertainty about who will be the substitute, for how long, and when the position will be permanently filled is an obstacle to learning—and it extends the emotional recovery period beyond what most adults expected. Throughout this transition, learning is being impacted.

When someone—and sometimes it is the substitute—is finally assigned, equilibrium can be restored. At least that is what most people, administrators, and parents would like to believe. However, if the reason for the former teacher's unexpected departure was never explained to the students, they may be left wondering what they might have done to cause their teacher to abandon them. On the surface, students may appear to be adjusting; but often their friendly welcomes and warm smiles are masks to shield students' doubts and their determination to avoid any missteps and risk losing another teacher. While many students seem independent and don't like showing vulnerability, losing a teacher can engender a sense of loss and abandonment. Administrators must stop viewing this as merely a staffing issue and understand that it impacts students' emotional development—and the efficacy of their learning environment.

Why Each Student Must Be Seen as a Whole Person

Classrooms are populated with children, teens, and young adults we refer to as "students." While it is convenient to refer to and treat them solely as "students," the developmental and maturational process experienced differently by each individual should make us appreciate the need for full-time, school-based, social and emotional resources for those we continue to fail to recognize as more than "students" to be assigned grades and shuffled between classes.

Similar to how we see those occupying seats in classrooms as one-dimensional "students," teachers who have been trained to provide instruction are insufficiently equipped to wear the multiple hats needed to actually address the range of social and emotional needs in their classrooms. The assumption has always been that once the doors are closed and instruction begins, every student has the capacity to—and will—self-regulate their behavior. They are expected to quietly cope with the mysteries of the natural developmental transformations they physically and emotionally experience, while consuming information on such subjects as algebra or the French Revolution.

This approach, which views students simply as containers conditioned to be recipients of academic information, neglects responsibility for the other experiences they internalize and interpret on their own and without guidance. We, as an education system, are bypassing the need to see them as whole individuals. Students need more than impersonal instruction that focuses on easily measured metrics. They need an education that nurtures their well-being and prepares them for the totality of their current and future lives.

In essence, rather than acknowledging the multidimensional people "students" truly are, schools conveniently evade being responsible for their overall well-being by viewing them through a one-dimensional lens. Without the benefit of professional training to equip teachers to understand and respond to the most fundamental, basic needs of developmentally diverse student populations, the current set of tools in every teacher's kit, particularly new teachers', is very limited and will impede their ability to effectively teach when pauses are necessary to respond to interruptions. If interruptions are caused by disruptive behaviors, the need to continue with lessons becomes the priority. Generally, the student's behavior is deemed the problem, and the course of action is to remove them from the class. And then what? To resolve the issue on their own while sitting on a bench outside of the principal's office? Of course, there is the added humiliation of being seen by other students, staff, and visitors to the school—all of whom usually interpret that any student sitting outside of the principal's office must have done something wrong. Having to anxiously await the principal's wrath, whether admonished politely or angrily, further compounds their circumstances. Fortunately, some principals are invested in at least hearing the student's perspective before determining whether any consequence is warranted.

When students have a behavioral issue, make those incidents teachable moments instead of punishable ones. View the incidents as social-emotional disruptions in need of a process that permits the student to work through whatever caused the problem. Students should be guided to learn appropriate ways to request time to speak with the school counselor or other qualified staff member who can help them navigate their way through whatever triggered their behavior.

So often we make the assumption that students arrive knowledgeable about and equipped to independently resolve conflicts related to stressful social or emotional situations. Even if and when those situations are of the students' own making, they should still have access to counseling. Otherwise, there will be a recurrence of disruptive behaviors in the future. But we need a process to more humanely address inappropriate or disruptive behaviors—not because we do not want a recurrence of those behaviors, but because students have to have some way to let us know they need help. They need guidance in understanding what they are experiencing, in learning ways to identify whatever initial signs begin to emerge that indicate they are about to have a problem, and in recognizing their options for how to deal with it.

Initially, all options should start with the assistance of a school counselor. When schools build in crisis-intervention counseling, it must be done on a short-term and long-term basis because student problems do not automatically disappear at the end of one intervention. It takes time to work through some of the more complicated issues they are contending with. But when students are extended invitations to seek help as needed, over time their awareness of the availability of support sends a message that they have no need to be afraid of whatever they are experiencing. Knowing they will not have to contend with their circumstances alone may have a calming effect. More importantly, when, during the tumultuous process of working through any crisis, students do not experience being judged for needing assistance, trust will be fostered between students and the school staff.

It makes sense to invest in resources throughout every developmental stage of a student's 13 years of attending school, because school is where they experience a life that naturally fluctuates through unexpected challenging moments. Our inability to acknowledge what is a part of the human condition at complex moments only exacerbates the circumstances. The irony is that when students misbehave, the first response—to discipline them—is also reprehensible. That is why, for the sake of every *child*-student, *teen*-student, and *young adult*-student, we have to recognize the human cost of not training teachers to monitor and attend to their students' social and emotional well-being, as it is likely to have a measurable impact on their academic performance outcomes. Widening the scope of what ought to be included in every student's educational experience is so critical to their overall educational experience.

Until our American education system adopts measures to attend to the developmental needs of the whole student, is it fair to trust the academic performance outcomes we rely on as indicators of growth in math, science and reading, when such areas as life skills are equally in need of growth to acquire confidence and competency? If we continue to ignore the impact of what students experience socially, we fail to see the true essence of a student's overall educational experience. They are not robots. What they produce academically cannot be measured or programed into an algorithm. Learning does not happen without the influence of what children, teens, and young adults socially and emotionally experience. What if academic failures in class are directly linked to stages of emotional imbalance; shouldn't we help students regain their social-emotional equilibrium and then proceed with their education?

Teachers need professional development training to recognize when students show signs of needing help. In addition to referring them to counseling, teachers also need to learn how to address failures that may be related to a student's academic performance. Reversing academic failure that is produced by non-academic-related circumstances needs to be addressed at the classroom level and with the support of a counselor. But the responsibility of recognizing when and how students may need non-academic support starts with teachers. The day-to-day interactions between teachers and their students put teachers in the best position to recognize signs indicating a change in a student's behavior. What to do about the signals related to a student's change in behavior is why specialists, professionally trained to coach teachers about how to assess the various levels of circumstances, are needed. The first priority is to train teachers about indicators representing different levels or types of behaviors. Then the next step is to have an awareness of what form of attention and intervention is needed. The frequency of students in crisis, as well as the type of crisis students experience while in school, is well beyond the ability of teachers and school administrators to manage without the assistance of full-time experts trained in psychology. If we want to influence teachers' decisions about whether or not to remain in the profession, then including full-time trained experts to help them navigate through incidents that result in meaningful resolutions is an absolute *must have*.

In some instances, how students perform academically precedes a student's act of behavioral frustration. If samples of student work reveal challenges being encountered, but the quality or method of instruction is not producing different results, it may be fairly safe to assume that handing back another paper with a failing grade could be the last straw. Professional development is needed to help teachers recognize signs of needing to improve their quality of instruction so they won't continually fail students. Although it is rarely acknowledged, teachers are not immune to experiencing educational fatigue and frustration. But, like their students, teachers *learn* how to become immune to their frustration. Embracing false claims, such as accusing students of not trying hard enough, is a very common practice. However, even when students are not trying hard enough, why is that an acceptable reason for not exploring alternative strategies to motivate them to try harder? After all, isn't that our job as educators? We should expect both students and their teachers to perform at the highest standards, but when neither students nor teachers are given resources to learn the skills necessary to achieve at the highest standards, all we are left with is aspirational rhetoric.

Consequently, all too often a new teacher's frustration is tied to not knowing how to handle their students' frustration with failing. When new teachers experience mounting frustration, and with no resources available to end their cycle of feeling like a failure, they start contemplating other options. If they decide to leave, it is the students' education that is put at greatest risk. In fact, from the moment the teacher decides to leave, the quality of instruction is further impacted because revolving doors that cycle-in a constant flow of replacements prevent any teacher from cultivating any semblance of a functioning classroom. Continuity of instruction is interrupted. In order for students to receive the best quality of education, their teachers will need to be retained to prevent disruption to learning continuity. If schools hope to retain teachers, they have to equip them with tools, strategies, and other resources to improve their quality of life in a highly demanding profession.

The goal of cultivating exceptional classrooms may be aspirational, but it has to be the standard. Retaining first-year teachers—with all of their promising potential—in classrooms will prevent students from losing valuable education time. The real danger is that, if we fail to categorize the departure of new and veteran teachers as a crisis in urgent need of attention, our lack of response will be reflected in the highest rate of low performance outcomes this country has ever seen.

Part 2: Transformational Staffing Model— Missing Links Unmasked

CHAPTER 4

Overview of Transformational Staffing Model

School-Based Professional Development Specialists

EVERY TEACHER IS RESPONSIBLE FOR THE PROGRESSION OF their students' education. That is an indisputable fact. As the process of supporting students along their learning curve depends on the teacher's degree of competency, nurturing each teacher's professional development is essential to maximizing their teaching potential. However, in today's classrooms, teachers don't have enough resources in their pedagogical tool kits to achieve their teaching potential. Lacking sufficient teaching resources in key areas impedes professional growth. When professional growth is impeded, teachers cannot gain competency in areas that impact every student's ability to prosper academically, socially, and emotionally.

To change the unsatisfactory status quo, we must imagine solutions beyond the current confines of narrow-minded and scarcity-based policies reflected in school budgets. Educational bias and faulty narratives about what low income and minority students are capable of achieving can be disproven by cultivating exceptional classrooms. The task of disproving biased perceptions that have negatively influenced the school budget process is possible by shifting the focus on realigning budgetary decisions with the new goals supporting what is in the best interest of each school. This book identifies a specific type of professional development that mirrors the resources most requested by teachers: assistance with classroom-related issues. Efforts to retain teachers need districts to hear and respond to their pleas for meaningful resources. Making their professional development needs a priority should be the most essential goal of every school budget.

To better grasp the conditions teachers work in, readers need to understand why the type of professional development proposed mirrors the support requested by teachers and why it matters most—including the purpose and predicted outcome of this particular professional development model, which is to support teachers in cultivating exceptional classrooms.

The missing links most essential to cultivating exceptional classrooms, and aligned with what teachers have spent decades requesting, are professional development experts to help them advance professional growth in six key areas: planning and delivery of instruction, knowledge of content, use of technology, inclusion practices, closure of learning gaps, and ability to effectively manage classrooms. The benefit of resources explicitly intended to support the professional development of every staff member, and particularly new teachers, is the multiple ways it will prove to be every school's greatest return on investment (ROI).

Transforming educational practices that will show measurable gains in student performance outcomes ought to be the core objective of every budget. Achieving the core objective will need strategic planning for training sessions at the school level. What is *not* needed are quarterly or monthly professional training sessions that gather teachers in obscure locations for a full day of wasted time. What *is* needed is school-based professional development experts capable of tailoring resources to the real needs of teachers at the classroom level. Embedding professional development resources in schools and making them available on a daily basis will transform and greatly improve the overall educational culture in every school. Expecting to achieve quality education without applying resources at the root level, inside every classroom, stunts the real potential growth of education for everyone. This new staffing model of professional support tied to specific classroom responsibilities has been the missing link teachers have needed to support their professional aspirations to deliver quality education. Reconstructing the paradigm of educational resources is an opportunity to set new priorities, making pathways to educational prosperity for all students far more possible when we institute practical and relevant professional support models. Educational prosperity is the standard for cultivating exceptional classrooms, particularly because it will greatly benefit the overall academic, social, and emotional well-being of every child, teen, and young adult.

The schools must be viewed as the second tier of a two-tier learning phase: the first phase is induction into the education profession in college teaching programs; the second phase is professional development guidance for all first-year teachers at the school level.

Resources Needed to Cultivate Exceptional Classrooms: A Reconstructed Teacher Training Paradigm

We accept the current paradigm of college education programs preparing teachers for careers in education. The common thinking has been that all teachers needed was to attend four years in an undergraduate program and then, if required by a state or school district, obtaining a teaching credential or enrolling in graduate school to earn a master's degree in education. But the reality of what awaits new teachers their first year in a classroom does call into question whether or not the current educational model sufficiently prepares new teachers. Within the first days of teaching, new teachers discover the gaps between the theories and principles taught in college and what actually occurs at the classroom level. When faced with the preoccupation of how to multitask their way through multiple challenges, including effectively managing a class while attempting to teach, many new teachers are flummoxed about what to do. Being in the midst of one conflicting moment after another, without knowing how to respond, is when first-year teachers discover the broad range of unexpected and challenging scenarios never addressed in college classrooms.

Being unprepared for the realities encountered at the school level makes their circumstances more dire. And that is why districts need to construct a new paradigm that focuses on adding another year of professional development training for newly hired first-year teachers. Schools and districts entice aspiring teachers who believe they will have wonderful careers in education. For so many, the short-lived dream of what could have been is overtaken by conditions that turn dreams into nightmares. While teaching may not be for everyone, it is a profession where way too many who are capable of teaching never get the chance to prove what they are capable of achieving, due to the conditions of the school culture and/or lack of adequate preparation (if any). It's really an unfair but totally fixable situation.

School-based professional development specialists are the resources needed to support the successful transition of first-year teachers from novice to proficient classroom leaders. The daily and direct support available to new teachers will bridge the gap between what teachers were taught in college and their real-world experiences while on the job. Post-college training programs in schools are the second tier of education needed to help teachers continue to progress along their professional learning curve. The value of this new training model is the additional benefit of using the classroom setting, making for the most realistic experience possible. College education programs are the first tier where the fundamental and foundational elements of education are taught. Students who successfully complete a degree program are eligible to qualify for teacher's licenses. The next stage of teacher preparation is for new teachers to use their first year as a full-time practitioner, cultivating their teaching skills at their place of work. Classrooms combined with the guidance of professional specialists are where teachers have the best opportunity to learn through on-the-job training. The true value of adding another year of education inside of a classroom setting is the benefit the experience will have on accelerating a teacher's professional growth and enabling them to flourish and gain competency.

The true value of the model is that teachers will benefit from receiving professional guidance to help them successfully navigate through the realities of life in the classroom. For example, learning how to deliver quality instruction is not something that happens in a vacuum. So often, attempts to deliver instruction are influenced by a variety of potential disruptions. Disruptions to the ebb and flow of class routines are quite common but often annoying because they interfere with each student's ability to maintain a focus on learning. Teachers can benefit from learning strategies for handling interruptions, including how to maintain control or recover from situations and then regain their instructional equilibrium to proceed with lessons. Successful recovery from interruptions, where issues are addressed followed immediately by the resumption of instruction, reflects well on the class' cultures.

Higher Education's Role in Preparing New Cohort of Professional Specialists

In the following chapters we will examine each specialist category in detail. First, let's consider the role of colleges and universities in preparing a new generation of professional development specialists for our schools. If we are invested in adding an additional year of professional development support for teachers at the school level, education and teaching programs at colleges and universities have to develop training programs to prepare experts needed to fill each professional development specialist position. Under ideal circumstances, teaching programs at colleges and universities would be strengthened in preparing content and instructional specialists for school-based support by utilizing the same educational resources that schools use, including curriculum standards. Given the span of curriculum standards that vary from state to state for all grade levels in our public schools, the absence of uniformity creates challenges for preparing specialists for instruction and content in college programs, as well as at the school level where the expertise of specialists is needed. Uniform curriculum standards across every state would enable some degree of continuity for schools and their students. However, given the current climate of proposed content and curriculum changes, based on divergent points of view; most of which are politically driven and meritless, now would not be an optimal time to decide on uniform standards across all states.

But for those of us who cling to the possibility of optimistic outcomes in the near future, issues addressing the lack of curriculum continuity have always been an area of concern. When students transfer to a new school during the school year, it is often a problematic experience. Transfers after the school year has begun, in many school districts, are complicated by a process that at best can be described as a free-for-all, where many schools across an entire state use different curriculums. In some communities, in the same town or city, sixth grade classes use different social studies books and schools or teachers get to choose the curriculum. Not only does the fact that different states use different curriculums complicate the process of students transferring from one state to another, but in some communities, there is no assurance that a sixth grader transferring from a math class in one school will be using the same math book upon their arrival to their new sixth grade class in another school in the same community. At a minimum, continuity in curriculum standards, as well as universal agreement of skills aligned with standards that need development across same grade levels, could greatly mitigate some of the current impediments faced by students transferring from one school to another. The emotional and social toll students have to contend with to assimilate with their new peers is challenging enough. Why should transitioning to a new school be additionally encumbered by confusion when assigned a textbook, educational materials, and other resources that do not match the curriculums used in their previous class?

There is no possibility of just picking up at their new school where they left off at their previous school. When they and their families receive their first report card from their new school, no one makes them aware of the possibility that a precipitous drop in grades could be attributed to instructional gaps. Instructional gaps are often due to topics or content not taught. When content is not covered, it becomes one of the primary contributing factors of learning gaps. Students transferring from one school to another, where there is minimal to no continuity in curriculum standards, are not the only ones impacted by instructional gaps. Common learning gaps are usually linked with instructional gaps. Elementary school principal Holly Elmore recommends that schools consider using Instructional Gap Analysis to remedy instructional gaps. Elmore describes the Instructional Gap Analysis as "a process that educators may follow in order to identify the gaps in instruction students have acquired as they move from one grade level to another." Her reasoning for schools to conduct Instructional Gap Analysis, where she makes clear that "schools need to know what students have been taught to be able to fill in the gaps in their learning," would be one solution for supporting all students, but particularly those transferring from one school to another (Educators Blog, GraduateProgram.org, August 27, 2021).

Addressing Instructional Gap Impediments

Schools should consider creating same-grade-level teaching networks, or instructional cohorts, to build continuity around curriculum standards and teaching practices across every subject area. Team collaboration will be strengthened if each grade level uses universally familiar concepts, curriculum standards, teaching practices, and educational resources. Commonly used assessments—including competency-based, academic-based, or performance-based rubrics with standards indicating students' degree of competency or level of understanding achieved—will foster cohesion around the uniform set of standards. Basically, normalization of collective pedagogical practices is what builds professional cohesion and helps first-year teachers become acclimated more quickly. All professional support specialists will be able to better support each staff member's individual professional growth in accordance with uniform grade-level standards. Over time, members of the network will develop habits supporting one another. Learning how to contribute to one another's professional growth as they learn the process of working collaboratively to achieve the same outcomes is how schools cultivate exceptional cultures.

Recent decisions by states to reverse course from their initial agreement to align with other states and use common curriculum standards for a few subjects will further complicate oversight and funding decisions by our federal public education system. Most states are in the process of drafting their own curriculum standards. However, it appears that they discovered the laborious process it takes to put in the time needed to create them from the ground up and may be opting to rename but keep a large portion of the current standards. That is helpful for preparing future teachers and professional development specialists assigned to practicum-internships in schools. For content and instruction specialists to succeed in their role, they must familiarize themselves with curriculum content and state standards at the state and district levels. Training professional development specialists to work with first-year teachers will close the gulf between teaching programs at the college level and the real responsibilities that await future teachers and other staff members at the school level. The new two-tier teacher training model will improve the quality of education because it will link college-degree graduates entering their first year of teaching with professional development specialists trained to develop and accelerate growth across the broad range of skills required of all new teachers.

Understanding the Limits of Standardized Assessments

Professionally trained experts brought to positions in schools will be interested in, and be expected to consume, data reflecting student academic performances. By default, most schools and districts tend to overvalue results in standardized assessments. Unfortunately, the level of universal acceptance for using those assessments and deeming the results as a reliable instrument for measuring student performance outcomes is a disservice to students and teachers. Why? Overreliance on standards-based assessment outcomes, as a determinative factor of what constitutes achievement, deserves a precautionary warning about one of the frailties of our education system. In general, many standards omit the importance of capturing a student's broader or future potential growth in areas beyond the limited boundaries tests are designed for. In the case of the now-universal practice of all students being required to take federally and state-mandated standardized tests, the practice of uniform assessments is predicated on the assumption that every student is equally capable of learning and processing information in the same way and at the same pace. That assumption is especially consequential to students receiving a substandard education in underperforming schools. But there are more far-reaching consequences that apply to all students.

Promoting one-size-fits-all tests is one of the essential errors of our entire public education system. When assessments are given, performance outcomes that result in a failing grade fail students unnecessarily. *Student performance outcomes are graded based on what they cognitively do or do not understand at the time they take any test.* But given the gravity of annual statewide standardized assessments, particularly in states where diplomas can be withheld and graduation plans derailed, it is unfortunate that students who perform "poorly" will bear the brunt of an inequitable and unfair testing system. Poor performances are an unwelcoming and embarrassing process that can potentially brand students as being intellectually substandard performers. And we wonder why dropout rates are increasing! Some forms of assessment are needed, but judging a student's performance outcomes based solely on a single test shows indifference towards skills in other areas in which students may be capable. Consider the real consequence of what the tests reveal. If a student fails, and then his or her teacher fails to address the failures, in the end we have to wonder who is failing whom; and what is the point of education?

Making Cognitive Development a Priority

If standardized assessments were divided into three stages, where the purpose is to find, assess, and then remedy errors, it would make for a more humane and educationally sensible process for all students. Instead, we humiliate students, who basically demonstrated what they had and had not learned. Performance outcomes ought to be treated as revelations of additional instruction needed. Instead, revelations are designated as worthy of passing or failing. And by the way, even students earning a passing grade ought to be given the opportunity to receive additional instruction and achieve proficiency or mastery. Student work that results in earning passing or failing during the initial round of correcting assignments is not good education practice. It's time we discontinue the practice of blaming and failing students. Why not use their performance results as *indicators reflecting current areas needing improvement, to advance a student's academic performance to proficiency status?* Or at least create a "comment" section to make clear, "The current grade is no indication of a student's future and overall capabilities; the outcome described simply captures the student's performance level at this moment in time." Education cannot be a system based on punishing or rewarding students. It ought to be used to, well . . . *educate students.*

The second stage, assessment, would require the development of a remedial plan to address learning deficiencies, rather than rubber-stamping a symbolically unfavorable status delivered with a sense of finality in an official document, which then is transferred into the student's official school record and embedded in the minds of those students assigned a failing grade. What a travesty! It is a travesty because it negates the maturational process of each student's individual pace of cognitive development.

Cognitive development, as defined in the simplest terms, centers around how an individual's brain learns how to think, problem-solve, and retain information. Reasoning, recalling learned information, and thinking are among the core group of cognitive skills connected with the brain. These and other cognitive skills are based on previous learning experiences that influence how we learn in the present and in the future. The key is to not allow the cognitive development process to stagnate. Cognitive growth is facilitated through degrees of challenging and rigor-based tasks that require higher-level problem-solving skills. As students ascend to each grade level, the volume of information and pace of how information is taught increase. The ability to store volumes of new and more rigorous information delivered at an increased teaching pace requires the continual evolution of one's learning capacity, fueled by the development of cognitive skills to advance their higher order of thinking skills.

Generally, it is assumed all same-grade-level students are capable of grasping, processing, and retaining information at the same pace. Therefore, the standard practice of utilizing uniform instructional methods to engage all students in learning the same way and at the same pace is a widely accepted practice. But it is problematic to make no allowances for differences in levels of development of cognitive skills among an entire student population in every grade level. Performance outcomes in annual reading and math assessments are reliable indicators that show not all students' cognitive skills develop at the same pace. However, it does not mean that a third grader who scored at the mid-level or lowest percentile is not capable of eventually achieving at the highest percentile in future grades. Cognitive development is not a uniform heterogeneous learning process.

We know many students are capable of recovering from the disappointment of receiving failing grades. But it's also true that many others who continually receive failing grades begin to convince themselves they are not smart enough to earn a passing grade. For them, the failing grade is not perceived as a missed opportunity to learn and master whatever they did not understand; Instead, their perspective is clouded by how to recover from the humiliation of receiving a failing grade. Fixating on failing grades—teaching students to take and accept whatever final grade appears on their assignment, rather than asking for additional instruction to learn and master concepts not understood—is not how we should frame the purpose of our education system.

I am not advocating taking out violins to elicit sympathy for students who earn failing grades. I'm simply proposing we mark student assignments with an invitation to meet with teachers for additional instruction, instead of assigning a failing grade. Educating students should always be about maximizing instructional opportunities that will give students the chance to achieve their true potential and bolster their belief that any obstacle can be overcome because they possess the ability to learn whatever is taught.

Teaching is so challenging because a commitment to helping students achieve learning proficiency requires an ability to devote quantities of time and additional instruction, both of which differ from student to student. The obstacles preventing teachers and students from engaging in meaningful learning time are too many to list. But it may be helpful to include protected learning blocks for one-to-one instructional sessions in each school day's schedule. Then we need to teach students how to learn to ask for additional support, or when they perfect the habit of dodging teachers to avoid attending tutoring sessions . . . please think of alternative approaches or times to meet. A useful incentive to include in the invitation might include food, music, arts and crafts, or a fun brain-teaser exercise to jump-start those sessions. It will help build a rapport of trust between teacher and student. Rapport is a valuable way of connecting with students who generally are ambivalent about meeting one-to-one with their teachers. But teachers must also understand that students generally feel apprehensive about spending more time mulling over mistakes in one of their least favorite subjects. After experiencing a few sessions that result in their ability to gradually produce better performance outcomes, the turning point occurs when they see evidence of what they are capable of achieving. The way we convince them why we never stopped believing in their ability to learn is to invest the additional time students need to develop learning skills that allow them to experience success. Since learning is associated with the pace of cognitive development growth that differs from one student to another, class instruction that is followed by individual one-to-one additional sessions may be a useful strategy for advancing cognitive development growth. The challenge is to identify instructional practices that will serve to unlock the true learning potential of every student.

The third stage is implementation of the remedial plan. It's also where professional development specialists are needed to work with teachers to draft a remedial plan and implement each step in the remedial process. The purpose of a transformative staffing model is not to perpetuate practices that no longer work or impede forward progress in advancing teachers' professional development skills. Instead, the purpose is to help teachers discover and utilize best practices to support their transition from novice to competent educators. Professionals knowledgeable in the most critical areas impacting the culture of classrooms will be instrumental in guiding teachers towards developing proficiency. Their assistance is key in helping new teachers acquire the skills needed to successfully meet the range of responsibilities required to deliver quality education to all students, and it will support underperforming schools in their transition to high-performing educational institutions.

Similar to teachers' needing to be considerate of each student's different learning pace, professional development specialists will need to understand how the same consideration applies to their cohort of students: the teachers and other professional staff members. Diverse learning profiles exist among students and teachers. It also matters to be aware of the difference in years and levels of experiences in how kids and adults process new information differently. Whenever opportunities exist for professional development specialists to expand a teacher's understanding of how cognitive development influences the way each student consumes, processes, and learns new information at his or her own pace, specialists should also impress upon the staff that the same applies to members in their cohort of professional educators. Teaching students or adults is its own learning process, because those on the receiving end of what is being taught need time to process new information. So the real lesson in teaching is that learning takes patience.

The Transformational Staffing Model in Action

Many teachers liken their day-to-day teaching experience to being alone on a deserted island. When challenges arise, they feel they are left to their own devices to figure things out. Too often, their SOS signals go unanswered, and they find themselves stranded with students who are depending on them. Without the proper tools and support, the teacher is unable to function as a leader in the classroom. Because I've seen these SOS flares ignored for too long, I've developed this transformational staffing model as a way to both validate teachers' concerns and provide workable pragmatic solutions that will have an immediate positive outcome in classrooms—and can be relied upon for multiple uses on future occasions.

Benefits for New Teachers

While all teachers need access to school-based professional development specialists, assistance may need to be prioritized based on each teacher's level of experience. In this approach, first-year teachers at the start of their teaching learning curve would receive more attention. It mirrors the equity in how learning time should be distributed in classrooms. Rather than instructional time being equally distributed to every student, proportionality of instruction should be tailored so that the amount of instruction is aligned with each student's level of need. If we see instructional time divided equally like slices of pizza, occasionally there will be students who require more one-to-one instructional time with the teacher—or a larger slice of the pie. First-year teachers are in a similar situation, so they may initially need more support in order to attain competency.

Currently, many schools assign veteran teachers to mentor new teachers (in addition to managing their own classrooms). This guidance is invaluable because it helps new teachers acclimate to the many responsibilities of their new role. With the help of mentors, new teachers can get acquainted with school routines, where to find classroom supplies, and protocols for supervising recess.

> *{Just as an aside, but an important FYI:* In many working-class and poor communities, classroom supplies are a scarcity. The generosity of teachers willing to personally purchase classroom supplies, including items like backpacks, is a standard practice for which most teachers receive little or no recognition. Their act

of kindness is worthy of appreciation because, on the first day of school, backpacks and other items placed on every student's desk are not usually among the supplies in any school's supply closet. Knowing their students' families may not be able to afford resources considered *must-haves* by students, so many teachers go the extra mile of using their personal funds to purchase school supplies. Aware of the unfair stigma low-income families may experience, compassionate teachers intuitively understand and prevent students from enduring the humiliating repercussions and shame of being *caught being poor*. Not being able to afford the most basic items, like a new backpack, which is regarded as an *essential* by all students, potentially pegs students as being among the lowest tier of socio-economic status. Because teachers recognize the importance of their students needing to make a positive first impression on their peers, some teachers opt to go the extra mile by purchasing and placing a brand-new backpack on the desk of every student, rather than a select few, to avoid even the potential of identifying any student's being perceived as a *have-not*. Any act of generosity that shows compassion by needing to consider equitable distribution of *must-have* items is worthy of another level of appreciation. It reflects a teacher's humanitarianism. Humanitarians make it clear that no student will ever feel a need to apologize for being poor.}

While new teachers are being mentored, informed about schedules and responsibilities related to bus duty and supervision of the cafeteria and recess, they also need their mentors to assist them with developing a rapport with other teachers and staff members. Orienting new teachers about their school's culture is necessary because the culture is greatly influenced by the level of collegiality among all staff members. Though veteran teachers are ideal mentors for orienting new teachers about school culture, their own teaching responsibilities preclude them from being available throughout the year to counsel and carefully guide a new teacher's professional growth in six key areas:

- Content
- Instructional Support
- Technology
- Classroom Management
- Inclusion Support
- Academic Achievement

Overview of Transformational Staffing Model

All of these are integral to the process of cultivating exceptional classrooms. The degree of availability of specialists for each of the key areas will greatly influence every teacher's ability to progress and achieve targeted competency benchmarks in their profession. Having school-based specialists available each day is how schools can effectively address the professional needs and growth of new teachers.

In order for first-year teachers to have a successful launch of their first days and weeks in their classroom, they should have at least a two-week training session with their specialist prior to the opening of the school year, to prepare for the opening day. Transitions into new jobs for any new employee take time. Specialists have to be cognizant of the natural state of nervousness first-time teachers are likely to have on their first day, which is why their first day should never coincide with the opening day of school for students. New teachers rightfully feeling jittery must not coincide with the anticipated jitteriness of their students on their first day of school.

As professional specialists guide teachers through their first encounters with the variety and volume of classroom and instructional preparations, they will need to avoid overwhelming new teachers with too much information in the early days. Skilled specialists will appreciate the similarities between new teachers and new students arriving to school on opening day. In many ways, new teachers, like their students, learn at their own pace, consume information in their own unique way, and need time and patience to master new information. In addition to possessing expertise in a particular subject or other area, specialists will need to be sensitive to how new teachers learn and process new information.

Students and teachers are sometimes expected to consume vast amounts of information in short periods of time, so portioning information into smaller consumable sizes may be advisable. When uncertainty occurs, or moments occur where new teachers inadvertently stumble and fall (such as making errors during instruction), specialists must train new teachers how to gracefully recover from these missteps. Teaching new teachers ways to revisit their mistakes, apologize, and share the correct information is an essential "best practice" that is critical to maintaining student trust within the classroom. New teachers have to be periodically reminded it's okay to make mistakes, but they also need to be equipped with ways to recover with dignity, grace, and sometimes humor.

In addition to reminding teachers that they are human and are prone to make errors, specialists must provide strategies for how to apologize for faux pas while being transparent about what was said and why it was incorrect. Showing teachers how to recover with grace in a room full of students will help new teachers show their human side and prepare them for inevitable moments of discomfort. A good strategy is usually just to be honest in a lighthearted manner. Cultivating classrooms where students encounter teachers as instructors—as well as normal people inclined to occasionally stumble—will help teachers be authentic role models. In addition, students will have the benefit of learning how adults publicly handle their mistakes. If we identify what all teachers, but especially new ones, need to advance their skills and achieve competency, and then give them the tools and support they require, fewer mistakes will occur. Errors made will not cover new teachers in a veil of shame. Similar to errors made by students that reveal areas in need of remedial support, professional support for new teachers will permit them to safely reveal areas they are in need of strengthening.

Honoring Veteran Teachers' Experience and Empowering Them Further

When professional development specialists are given the honor of working with veteran staff members, they should be considerate of the range and depth of experience each has accumulated. Showing deference to veteran teachers, who have had to endure a career without the benefit of professional resources, will not be listed among the responsibilities for each specialist. But it may help to keep in mind the journey they've had to travel. Most veteran teachers have had to learn how to stay afloat while constructing their own lifejackets or learn survival skills once they landed on a deserted island without access to resources. Whether stranded at sea or on an island, the new staffing model is the lifeline most teachers have been waiting for.

One way of assessing a veteran teacher's level of need is to confer with them about the current instructional practices they use. It would be useful to begin with creating clusters of teachers at each grade level, and then inquire about the methods and practices they have used that have garnered successful outcomes. Respecting the years of work veteran staff members have dedicated themselves to, before making assumptions about what they need to improve their performance outcomes, conveys that even qualified professional specialists can learn from those who already possess exceptional teaching skills.

In the initial phase of collaborating with teachers, starting discussions related to their experiences will create the conditions for constructive dialogue. Invitations to share an inventory of best practices they currently use individually, but which were previously unknown among their colleagues, can be embedded with show-and-tell topics for all future meetings. Including current best practices used by staff members will help build ownership of a new professional-development model. Successfully launching training sessions and gaining acceptance by all staff members starts with building trust, both among one another as colleagues and between staff and specialists. Prioritizing trust-building will reduce staff members' apprehensions about working with experts.

Any new process can be successfully initiated by engaging with those you were sent to assist in their professional growth, by recognizing, first and foremost, their individual comfort zones. Intuitively savvy educators have learned to be dubious or skeptical about others who they were told were qualified in professional development positions but whose skills turned out to be well below what they were led to expect. Among these seasoned educators, credibility of qualifications matters greatly.

Respecting where first-year and veteran teachers are, across the spectrum of teaching experiences, should also be taken into account. New first-year teachers may need support in building their professional skills from the ground up. Newly assigned teachers who transfer from one school to another school deserve to be differentiated from the first-year teachers. Often, seasoned teachers voluntarily applying to open positions in new schools possess qualifications similar to those of their new veteran colleagues. If they were recruited by the school, it is the highest form of respect a competent teacher can earn.

Therefore, while first-year teachers are likely to need support to advance their status as novices, qualified and experienced veteran teachers with established reputations, who are performing at much higher competency rates, will likely benefit from support that builds out their current practices. Building out is a process of finding ways to add strategies by tweaking or refining techniques they already use. Basically, when support specialists encounter commendable teaching practices, they can offer ways to expand the current practices where needed. A great way to recognize contributions and foster collegiality is to catalog verified successful teaching practices of veteran members of each grade-level collaborative and distribute them among every member in the group; both will positively impact school culture.

All specialists should approach their work with a sense of how to balance the responsibility of advancing professionals at every level along their learning curve, while deferring to their wisdom. Often, teachers have independently acquired their skills through years of devotion and dedication to a profession that takes so much energy and time, and yet they persistently give for the sole purpose of doing their utmost to educate students well. Even underperforming schools have teachers dedicated to improving outcomes. It's important to be receptive to them and without judgment of the conditions they inherited but remain dedicated to doing their best to improve. Whatever condition school cultures are in, professional development specialists must refrain from passing judgment in the initial stages of developing partnerships with every teacher, staff member, and school leader, since they likely inherited and then were not adequately resourced to change the conditions. The intent of all specialists has to start with an appreciation for the circumstances requiring every school staff member to work doubly or triply hard, due to the scarcity of quality educational resources in their school. Despite being in a fragile state from ongoing threats of closure or enduring demeaning publicity about assessment outcomes, specialists were brought there to work with a staff desperately in need of their support to overcome the very same hurdles that have contributed to the many years of substandard conditions at their school. An infusion of professional development support at the school level will be a monumental change and lead to qualitatively measurable improved performance outcomes for teachers and their students.

One word of caution may be needed here regarding the tendency to automatically assume that the degree of professional support that specialists offer should be based on the number of years one teaches. The need is straightforward when it comes to first-year teachers, but many veteran teachers have never had the benefit of professional development support to advance their competency in the range of responsibilities expected of every teacher. Although they may be endowed with more experience, the years of experience are not a true indication of a veteran teacher's level of mastery. They too may need professional development support to improve their instructional skills—or skills in the other areas proposed for specialist training. The correlation between gaps in teaching performance competency and student academic achievement gaps applies to every staff member responsible for teaching students.

Working Toward Measurable Outcomes

We no longer need to continue researching "causational" factors contributing to poor quality of life among generations of poorly educated students from childhood to young adulthood and throughout their adult years. We already know what caused those conditions. It's way beyond time to shift our focus from inquiries about the *why* and resolve to address *how* educational inequities can be fixed. Implementing the transformative staffing model is a first step in that direction.

Shifting to a new staffing model that makes teachers and school staff the central recipients of professional development resources will provide practical opportunities to address learning gaps. This model will help schools cultivate new norms that no longer passively allow students to experience degradation from failure. Instead, students will benefit from their teacher's ability to use instruction as the remedy for learning deficiencies, potentially removing the fear of failure for both teachers and students.

In this environment, students and teachers will no longer view failing grades as personal failures. It's time to remove the shame that comes when students make errors. Teachers will draw comfort from knowing there are strategies and protocols for remedying errors, and students' self-esteem will increase because they will have the opportunities and skills to master the content and concepts that they previously found challenging. Teachers and students will benefit from exposure to diverse methods of instruction. In turn, learning gaps that are detected by teachers will become learning *objectives* for students (rather than signs of student failure).

Focusing on transforming learning gaps into learning opportunities will also give schools the chance to shift away from perpetuating unfair stereotypes that blame students for poor academic performance outcomes. When teachers have the resources to be successful educators, they will be able to cultivate academically successful students who will defy low expectations and patently false assumptions.

All adults in schools need the right kind of tools and resources to convert failing educational institutions into what schools were always intended to be—and in some communities are—places committed to ensuring every student is well equipped with the necessary learning tools that will result in educational prosperity. Students' achieving educational prosperity is how we restore parents' and students' faith in an educational system that has enacted inequitable and unfair policies for generations. The addition of school-based professional development specialists has been among the missing links teachers and school staff have needed to fulfill the mission of making it possible for every student to achieve educational prosperity and make good on the commitment to leave no child behind.

Having professional experts available to advance each teacher's understanding and overall competency is essential in helping teachers stop thinking and responding to students' lack of understanding as being worthy of nothing but a failing grade. Professional specialists are a lifeline for teachers because their professional partnership will focus on helping students master concepts by acquisition and continued strengthening of learning skills.

Fully engaging students in lessons requires a comprehensive instructional model designed to capture and sustain the attention of students who represent a cross section of different-leveled learners with diverse learning profiles. This by far is the most important reason instructional specialists in schools will benefit teachers in need of assistance in learning about the value of using various methods of instruction aligned with diverse learning profiles.

Best Evidence: Students Master Learning

Learning deficiencies that have been ignored eventually lead to ongoing cycles of learning gaps. Corrective measures for addressing learning gaps proposed in my previous book, *America's Educational Crossroads*, include a road map for detecting and addressing learning gaps. Some of the remedies for learning gaps may be linked directly to instructional gaps. A teacher's tool kit of instructional teaching practices, also referred to as *methods of instruction*, will be expanded by the support of an instructional specialist capable of introducing teachers to ways to construct lessons to fully engage all students in learning. Embedding professional support specialists to improve the quality of instruction in schools is how we can distribute meaningfully strategic remedies at both ends of the learning spectrum. Placement of strategic educational support at the starting point of a student's educational journey will greatly contribute to reducing the number of students experiencing learning deficiencies that lead to learning gaps. Imagine being able to reduce the percentage of students needing a remedial plan in each class by placing instructional resources at the starting end of the spectrum. Basically, evidence will show how impactful decisions to avail resources to teachers in classrooms at the beginning of a school year can lead to not only a reduction in learning gaps and student referrals for remedial plans to close gaps, but a reversal of poor performance outcomes.

When trends show consistent cycles of learning success in schools where high numbers of their student population previously performed at substandard levels, the improved rates of academic success can be attributed to the resources provided to teachers and staff members working in collaboration with experts to improve the quality of instruction. Conversely, if resources are denied to teachers at the start of the school year and/or as needed during the rest of the year, then the result will be a gradual increase in remedial plans for closing achievement gaps. Measures to improve teacher competency in all areas, but particularly in instruction, is how we open pathways to students' mastering learning of content.

Educational Excellence Links Quality Teaching to Student Learning

Achieving mastery of content is equivalent to demonstrating educational excellence. Students who demonstrate educational excellence are those who routinely perform and then are recognized and rewarded with the highest grades. When they maintain that level of performance, they earn the status of being among the elite. Their names appear on their school's honor roll, where they are likely to be chosen for valedictorian or salutatorian. Students who perform near or within range of the highest academic performers are acknowledged and rewarded with scholarship offers to college. Having institutionalized a process of an educational class system gives the appearance that tiers of performance outcomes are both preordained and a settled matter. It's a microcosm of our societal class system where a majority of America's economically poorest also are among the highest population of students poorly educated.

Occasionally, when students who live in poor communities unexpectedly show signs of educational promise, they are recipients of additional attention; generally, by being worthy of more teaching time and access to additional resources. It is how our education system marks students for future success. Students who are perceived to possess innate learning ability often are designated as being "worthy" of acknowledgment and additional support. Being deemed "worthy" of additional attention can come in a variety of forms, including receiving compliments about being naturally gifted, or being informed about possessing exceptional learning attributes. Any and all forms of praise fuel a student's self-esteem, which ignites their educational aspirations and serves as motivation to apply greater effort to achieve at the highest standards. Most notably, the positive feedback convinces them to believe in their capabilities. Imagine how other students would be motivated to achieve if they were recipients of a steady diet of being told, "You possess the ability to do well," combined with additional assistance to succeed. Students of all ages are highly impressionable and have a tendency to believe what they are told.

Unfortunately, we've settled on the status quo, accepting an inequitable education class system that accepts a diverse range of performance outcomes. The normalization of differing levels of education performances, from failing to barely passing, demonstrates how students readily accept their status along our system of grading on a bell curve. Too many students are subject to performance apathy, where they learn to apply a level of effort based on what influential adults raised them to believe they were capable of achieving. The eradication of performance tiers in our education system needs a solution that targets acquisition of learning skills for all students. Rather than accepting a failed and inequitable system that has been purposefully constructed to reward the few, we can optimize the educational success of a vast number of students across the entire spectrum by linking each student's capacity for achieving educational excellence with quality instruction that unlocks every student's true ability to learn. Until now, it has been a challenge to divest from the current educational tier system, where acceptance of average to below-average and failing performances is the norm, because of our failure to come up with a solution. But now we have one.

This solution is likely to lead to greater numbers of valedictorians and salutatorians and no students who fail. If we commit to a process of reconstructing the process of educating students by targeting the need to acquire learning skills, we can in fact achieve what should have always been America's optimal education objective: to give every student a chance to show their ability to perform at high standards. Mastering learning skills in something as basic as reading is essential for comprehending content as well as expanding knowledge. The ability to process information across all content areas that is presented at higher and more rigorous levels at each ascending grade level, is how new knowledge is acquired. But the continual acquisition of higher learning skills, which enable the continual growth of knowledge, requires a high degree of mastery.

For mastery to be achieved among students, we must retool teachers with new instructional skills. Retooling teachers must be driven by a philosophy that sees the capacity of all students to learn. But if we really want to divest from one practice by adopting a different philosophy and retooled instructional practices, both have to be supported with professional specialists at every school to help teachers obtain new expected educational benchmarks. By providing teachers with the professional development support they desperately need, we will help them reach their professional potential so that students can achieve their educational potential. Then the education system will be able to evaluate professional growth accurately and fairly. Benchmarks aligned with verifiable measurable performance standards will be an indicator of effective teaching—and every teacher evaluation will include goals for attaining competency in closing academic gaps.

How We Ensure Attainment of Improved Professional Performance Outcomes

Accountability of the transformational staffing model, and its mission of elevating competency to levels of proficiency among all school staff members, can be judged based on the performance outcomes of teachers and staff members. Additional evidence of whether and to what degree the professional resources provided actually made a difference also has to be reflected in student performance outcomes. Therefore, a plan is needed to monitor and fairly access the level of effectiveness proposed, as justification for adopting the new staffing model. But please refrain from making any final determination at the conclusion of just one school year.

Modifications may need to be made, but since it realistically may take new teachers anywhere from three to five years to show meaningful growth results, withholding any judgment of whether to value and proceed with the newly proposed staffing model warrants retaining the support system throughout a cycle of at least three to five years.

By the end of the first year, one way of measuring the effectiveness of the model is to count the number of first-year teachers who remained throughout the entire school year. Then ask them if they intend to remain the following school year. If every new teacher remains, it may be one of the strongest indicators that the model has merit. If any teacher decides to depart during the school year, ask them to share their reasons for their decision in an *exit interview* with a neutral and trusted person. The interview questions should include their assessment about the professional development resources provided. Find out whether or not those resources were helpful. If they were not seen as helpful, delve a little further to discover why. Accountability that welcomes transparency by inviting open and honest favorable and unfavorable responses will add to the integrity of the mission. But real integrity will be earned by responding to the feedback by addressing the unfavorable. Teachers who choose to remain should participate in a *retention interview*. What those who intend to remain share about their experiences as a first-year teacher is valuable. Their input can serve as an assessment about the level of effectiveness of specialists' performance. There may be a combination of praises and criticisms, all of which should be documented and shared with whomever the praise and/or criticism applies to. Specialists, like the teachers and staff members they serve, should be extended the time and grace needed to improve their performance. In some cases, this may require changes and time to work through issues to strengthen areas in need of improving.

Assessing the impact of the new staffing model needs to extend accountability to teachers and staff members. Measuring performance outcomes of teachers and other staff members, to determine whether or not the new staffing model holds value for them, should be done through a process that is perceived as aspirational and without judgment. The primary focus should be a humane system that places emphasis on the teacher's or staff member's professional growth towards developing proficiency relative to their assigned responsibilities. Implementation of an Exceptional Classroom Plan that is designed collaboratively with teachers can foster comfort among them by welcoming and including their input. Naming the plan an Exceptional Classroom Plan places the onus of what the plan is intended for—cultivating exceptional classrooms—directly on efforts to improve the overall culture of the classroom environment and not on each teacher in a personal way. Avoiding targeting teachers on a personal level will likely reduce the probability of their feeling defensive. Lowering the perception of holding them personally responsible is achievable by emphasizing ways to improve specific areas linked with helping them develop their professional growth so they can be the lead agent of positive changes. While the Exceptional Classroom Plan is contingent on promoting each staff member's individual professional aspirations for achieving competency at a level of proficiency, the overarching goal is to benefit their students.

The Exceptional Classroom Plan

Every professional specialist can work with teachers and staff members to gather baseline information about their current performance level for areas they are assigned, to assist teachers and staff with their professional growth. The purpose is to use an openly transparent process to query and discuss with school staff and teachers their perspectives through self-assessment of strengths and areas they think need improving. The importance of teachers and other staff members contributing to the process of creating a general baseline of their professional profile, showing where they currently see their skills, will be useful in developing a professional plan designed for them and with them to improve their skills. Capturing each staff member's baseline of competency from their point of view in the initial stages of collaboration will help to establish a professional relationship.

Initial visits to the classroom will help specialists gather additional baseline information of a staff member's performance. For the sake of maintaining full transparency, whatever new information is gathered, the specialist must meet with and share their findings with the staff member before proceeding to the next step in drafting an Exceptional Classroom Plan. It is vital to first cultivate trust before identifying goals for the plan. Goals need to be aligned with clear objectives that staff members clearly understand prior to moving forward. The implementation of the plan is the responsibility of teachers and their support staff. To achieve specified goals in the plan, cohesion, continuity, and consistency among all staff involved are essential in implementing the Exceptional Classroom Plan. School staff members also need to agree to subsequent steps, including a system to track progress toward achieving goals. Other elements of the plan include benchmarks delineating desired growth as a measurable sign of progress within specific periods of time. The idea is to train staff members to maintain their focus on developing the skills that will gain them proficiency and advance their level of performance to full competency.

Incentivizing ongoing participation for school staff in many ways mirrors what they should do when working with their students to help them believe in the possibility of achieving their educational aspirations.

The purpose is to chronicle milestones achieved and areas in need of strengthening, but to do so without judgment. Everyone tends to listen better when messengers find ways to communicate respectfully. In fact, communication style greatly influences every phase of the plan's implementation process. Chronicling progress of milestones achieved, sharing areas in need of strengthening, providing specificity of strategy and resources used, visiting classrooms, observing the culture of classroom routines, and consulting with teachers all are intended to result in measurable outcomes. But outcome results can be derailed by style and manner of communication. Every specialist must possess a level of fundamental communication skills that convey their role and intention of being the best advocate of each teacher's professional development growth. Doing that well builds a healthy professional alliance. After investing in the new transformational staff model, district and school leaders should look for and carefully scrutinize evidence of improved proficiency by each school's staff members. Progress can be measurable and independently verified. The best evidence will be seen in the increased level of a teacher's confidence, in the competency skills they have acquired, and in the overall improved academic performances of their students.

CHAPTER 5

Content Specialist

WHEN MOST PEOPLE THINK OF EDUCATION, THEY THINK about the core content areas that have been the focus of classroom instruction for generations: reading, writing, and arithmetic. Add to that science and history. We tend to focus on the more traditional content areas, and though there's much more that students need to learn to be successful, we'll start with focusing on the need for multiple on-site content specialists to represent each content area in the new transformative staffing model. But first, let's explore the everyday classroom realities that make content specialists a necessary part of rebuilding our education system.

Content Instruction Today

Currently, our public education system relies on ensuring guaranteed compliance with laws requiring teaching and school-leadership certification. Periodic renewal of professional licensing is done through an application process. Licensing policies are intended to ensure a level of qualification is met in accordance with standards adopted by each state and approved by the federal government in the 2001 No Child Left Behind education law. The 2001 law was the hallmark of a promise to leave no child behind.

On so many occasions, several school districts have fallen short of keeping that promise when it comes to teacher qualifications. Unfortunately, assigning teachers to courses they are not certified to teach pales in comparison to the number of districts that fill leadership roles with unqualified and unlicensed individuals allowed to manage schools or departments. Many are mystified about how those officials manage to completely evade taking the required exams within the timeframes everyone else is expected to abide by. What deepens the mystery further is that, when inquiries are made about the reasons for unlicensed leaders, the responses given are just another form of obfuscation. And another promise not kept.

What does this disconnect between teacher qualifications and actual duties look like in classrooms? Many people are unaware of the degree of cooperation, accommodation, and flexibility that is expected of teachers. For example, in some schools, teaching assignments vary from one year to the next. Veteran teachers licensed and fully certified to teach math or science may arrive at school and be informed that, due to a staffing shortage, they have now been assigned to also teach a history class. The fact that this teacher has no experience in teaching history doesn't seem to matter to school administrators. They need to fill positions in order to be—at least on paper—in compliance with government-mandated rules, even if they must use teachers who are untrained to teach those subjects. That is the reality our students live with. Of course, this only serves to further diminish the reputation of our entire education system.

In our communities, so little is known about the practice of randomly assigning teachers, with little or no notice, to teach in areas they were untrained in or in which they do not possess a certified license to teach. This exposes another truth about the lack of enforcement of the federally and state-mandated policies. Across the country, policies are not enforced equitably. Often, because district budgets have been defunded, school leaders circumvent policies by finding ways to work around weightless state regulations.

Even when teachers are assigned to teach content in which they are certified and licensed, it is assumed that they are capable of providing quality instruction. It may come as a surprise to hear that many educators fail to understand the distinction between *knowledge* about content and *knowing how to teach* content. Familiarity with content is not an indicator of possessing instructional proficiency. The current practice of hiring new teachers without a professional development plan reveals two erroneous assumptions: they arrive possessing enough knowledge about the content, and they are familiar with the instructional methods needed to be a successful teacher.

In order to prepare teachers for success, we need to first differentiate knowledge of content from knowing how to teach the content. Equally important is the need to recognize that simply possessing basic knowledge of content is insufficient. The potential for stagnation is likely if we do not value the importance of continued growth to remain current with advanced information more readily available. Learning ways to link contemporary content resources with lessons enriches curriculum and provides a more well-rounded education experience for students. Failure to provide funding results in reliance on outdated educational resources. Use of outdated curriculum deprives teachers of opportunities to include a broad array of content resources reflective of the wealth of current information available, particularly discoveries and updates of findings and facts previously unknown. We need our curriculum to be contemporary and framed within a broader context to include national and global events, as well as insights and diverse perspectives.

Professional content specialists knowledgeable about the volume of current resources related to their specific subject of expertise are needed to expand and enrich each teacher's meta-library of content resources. Outdated traditional content resources have to be replaced with contemporary resources. By way of example, high school history classes should include, but not stop at, teaching students about America's Industrial Revolution. A historical chronology of events should be presented with timelines that include how countries have evolved since the landmark events that altered the nation's cultural and political landscape.

Also, historical events generally don't occur in a vacuum. In many countries, examination of factors that preceded each evolution or revolution is warranted, for students to gain an appreciation of how they impacted outcomes of those events many years, decades, and centuries later. If we remain inside of textbooks with chapters divided into units describing the French Revolution, assigned on pages 21–41, taking students through an abbreviated version of that period, and then ignore how the nation of France was forever changed—and what those changes have been, subsequent to the war—we are doing a disservice to how students are educated. What is the purpose of studying history if we contain events inside of books with little opportunity for students to learn about and discover how events of the past shape current government, policy, and commerce, as well as other decisions occurring today? We make so much of "children being important to the future," yet we fail to really prepare them for their future. It is often said that history has a way of repeating itself. But does it necessarily have to? Teachers are the instruments of facilitating instruction. There will be added value when teachers expand their encyclopedia of historical and contemporary knowledge about the content they teach. Expanding their knowledge of content enriches curriculum and lessons, and that is the primary goal of content specialists tasked with assisting teachers' progress in that area.

Bridging the Gap with Content Specialists

Providing teachers with daily in-person access to dedicated content development specialists will improve the overall quality of content taught in all classes. In the transformational staffing model, there will be six content specialists in each school, and they will each be highly qualified in a specific category: math, sciences, language arts, history, financial literacy, and technology (computer science literacy, digital literacy, and information literacy).

Each of the six content specialists must demonstrate a depth of knowledge about the content, a deep familiarity with grade-level standards and skills targeted for development, and a librarian's diverse catalog of resources, including verifiably credited traditional and contemporary content sources. Because content specialists are experts in their area of focus, they will be able to vet curriculum resources and help teachers access a broad and credible range of materials.

The first step for content specialists will be to assess each teacher's current baseline knowledge of the content area they have been assigned to teach. The departmentalization of courses by subject areas at the middle and high school levels will make the collaboration between teachers and content specialists less challenging than elementary schools, where teachers may be assigned multiple subjects to teach. One possible way to bypass scheduling complications, where one teacher is responsible for teaching multiple subjects, is to group teachers into working clusters for each content area. The benefit of each content specialist's working with a nucleus of same-grade-level teachers teaching the same subject is the opportunity to build teams to foster professional collaboration, where team members contribute to the progression of their colleagues. Content specialists will still work one-to-one with individual first-year teachers, and veteran teachers as needed, to support their progression towards achieving competency in knowledge and expansion of resources related to area(s) of content they have been assigned to teach.

In addition to advancing each teacher's depth and breadth of subject knowledge, content specialists must also possess detailed knowledge of their district's curriculum standards. This will enable them to distill the information and guide teachers' understanding of strategies that align knowledge of grade-level content with skills targeted for development in curriculum standards.

As content specialists support teachers in expanding their knowledge of content areas, they also show teachers how to effectively deliver content across diverse educational platforms specific to each content area. Given the range of demands classroom teachers already contend with, it is invaluable to support their professional growth by having content specialists available to research, catalog, and disseminate relevant findings related to specific topics planned for instruction. In this way, content specialists become the conduit between teachers and instructional resources. Specialists will be uniquely qualified to curate a library of vetted resources that will enhance teachers' knowledge, which then is embedded in lessons that enrich the quality of education provided to students. This ensures that students are being taught up-to-date information that reflects each field's best practices.

The ultimate measure of success for content specialists and the teachers they support will be whether the teachers' content mastery is successfully transferred to students. In other words, teachers' proficiency will be evaluated based on the success of their students. When students meet high academic standards, we will know that the specialists and teachers assigned to them have done quality work. And as teachers experience more successful outcomes, they can collaborate with each other and with content specialists to establish new best practices at the classroom level.

For more about the roles and responsibilities of the content specialist, see page 176 in the appendix.

CHAPTER 6

Understanding the Convergence of Content and Instruction

PROGRESSION ALONG CONTENT LEARNING CURVES COINCIDES with an ability to teach. Too often, teaching positions are filled with people definitely knowledgeable about content but lacking in how to teach it. Deficiencies in instruction are most often revealed during classroom observations, particularly in unscheduled visits. Scheduled or unscheduled observations sometimes occur in response to assessments shared by those most impacted: the students. Student complaints about experiencing a disconnect in understanding what is being taught are usually overheard in common public spaces such as hallways and cafeterias. Whether grumbling out loud and in open spaces about what they experience is intentional, students know that if colleagues of the teacher they are dissatisfied with are within hearing range, their complaints will be heard.

If complaints are overheard, it is a mistake for the listener to assess whether or not the people making the complaint are regarded as disgruntled students known for having disruptive behaviors, which in turn devalues the legitimacy of what they reveal. It is worth taking their complaints seriously. Why? If no steps are taken to defuse the situation, it could fester into a bigger problem. The reputation of student behaviors may or may not be indicative of their experience in a particular class. Sometimes disruptive or rude behaviors exhibited by students can be a manifestation of frustration linked with the lack of success experienced in one or more classes. But even students who consistently perform at high passing levels can be disgruntled by what they perceive as inadequate instruction. Either way, the situation has to be defused at the earliest stage to prevent bigger problems.

School leaders who make an effort to routinely visit classrooms on a weekly basis, but especially at the beginning of each year, can get a baseline understanding of each classroom's culture. Indicators of classroom culture can include observing how the teacher conducts him or herself during instruction, as well as getting a sense of the operational ebb and flow of routines. But a more impactful indicator of classroom culture is the quality of interactions between teacher and students, as well as social interactions among students. Without visiting classrooms, school leaders miss opportunities to convey to their staff members and students how much they value witnessing the process of how diligently teachers work to deliver exceptional teaching to cultivate a learning environment inclusive of all students.

If and whenever teachers fall short of meeting performance benchmarks, or there is a need to take students' concerns about a disconnect between what is being delivered and how well or poorly it is understood, the presence of professionally trained specialists available to support teachers in need of expanding their knowledge about the content they teach, and/or trained in instructional strategies to improve their quality of instruction, will enable detected inadequacies to be addressed. Instead of teachers' being conditioned to fear shortcomings in areas needing strengthening to enable continued progression towards competency, their having immediate and direct access to trained experts will advance the school's culture by enshrouding every teacher's confidence in the reassurance that all problems have solutions. Novices' skills do not need or deserve to be judged as inadequate. All beginners start their career at a natural stage of infancy. If left without access to resources that can propel their growth, then understandably their performance level will stagnate at the stage where most beginners start. Intervention in the way of professional support is essential to the educational development and well-being of teachers and students.

Either way, there will be a need to invest in efforts to prove or disprove complaints about what students experience. Whenever there is merit to complaints by students, it generally reflects the potential of colliding factors: either the teacher is sufficiently knowledgeable about the content but demonstrates inadequate experience in an ability to teach; or the reverse—the teacher knows how to teach but demonstrates insufficient knowledge about the content. When students express frustration with an inability to grasp information because of the way it is being taught, then administrative visits—early and often—to those classrooms are warranted. Administrative visits, however, are not the remedy for whatever needs to be addressed.

School leaders' unfamiliarity with strategies for improving the quality of a teacher's instructional skills is a fairly common conundrum. It is why they either hire professional development specialists to do in-school trainings a few times during the year or turn to qualified veteran staff members to periodically run professional development sessions. Both models lack in classroom visits to assess conditions, schedule weekly training sessions to advance the teacher's instructional skills, and observe the delivery of new instructional methods.

Currently, school leaders may assess areas in need of improving and then recommend improvements, but often not included in documents are the *how* and *where* one can turn to for assistance in advancing teaching skills. Districts that identify specified professional resources to address instructional gaps, can only recommend but not force teachers to accept or invest in supports available to help them develop competency in the recommended areas specified. Pursuant to agreements between school districts and teachers' unions, where the rights of union members are clearly delineated and fully protected, teachers who refuse to engage in professional development services but are also within their right to remain in the position the following year, can hinder the progress of educating students. In this instance, the potential perils of a grading system decided by teachers who demonstrate incompetency in any area, but particularly in the ability to teach, is deeply problematic.

Discrediting report-card grades students and their families feel were punitive and based entirely on the poor chemistry between a student and teacher, or disagreeable interactions between family members and the teacher, can be avoided by including school-based specialists to help inexperienced and experienced teachers develop better teaching skills. Deconstructing a series of barriers—including how to respond to students expressing concerns about the quality of instruction, observations concluding that the level of instruction demonstrated by a teacher warrants attention, or occasionally the need to bypass policies that benefit union members but hinder advancing any student's education to enable their ability to continue progressing along their learning curve—can be achieved through the addition of school-based qualified professional specialists.

There are other obstacles that cannot be overlooked, if cultivating exceptional classrooms can be achieved with the addition of new staffing positions. Structurally, elementary school classrooms operate differently from middle and high schools. One obvious difference is in the range of courses elementary teachers are responsible for teaching. For many of those teachers, being knowledgeable about the broad range of subjects, as well as planning lessons and providing instruction, has proven to be very challenging. Elementary teachers would find, and likely appreciate, working with specialists to help them better manage the enormous weight of expectations they inherit.

In middle and high school, many believe teachers have the advantage of being responsible for teaching subjects within a specific discipline, such as math, science, or humanities. Currently, a majority of elementary schools operate using an instructional model where the majority of lessons occur in self-contained classrooms; and with the exception of music, art, and gym classes, all subjects are taught by the same teacher most of the school day.

At the elementary school level, teachers authorized to teach multiple subjects have a Multiple Subject Teaching Credential. While several may have stronger preferences for some subjects over others, they are required to equally divide the instructional time across all subjects they are responsible for teaching. At least that is the expectation. Equal time given to instruction, however, does not necessarily mean equal passion or time will be devoted to planning lessons in subjects least preferable over those most preferred. Often, the level of enthusiasm for teaching some subjects is evident in the level of passion a teacher displays while teaching them. Sometimes, the less-preferred subjects might even receive less instructional time. The noticeable dip in enthusiasm during instruction of less-preferred subjects is often equal to the reduced amount of time teachers devote to preparing for that subject. If teachers were provided access to professional experts knowledgeable about both content and instruction, they would then advance their instructional skills while deepening their knowledge about content they are responsible for teaching. It would also help reduce the amount of apprehension elementary teachers feel about possessing strength in some subjects, while needing to strengthen instructional skills in other subjects.

Teachers who demonstrate the ability to teach but lack knowledge about subjects they are assigned to teach cannot be expected to achieve exceptional academic performance outcomes. And yet this is a situation too many teachers are placed in across many schools and districts. Another example of teachers experiencing the *"Wait! You want me to teach what subject?" Fear Syndrome*, is a common occurrence during unexpected staffing shortages. Actually, given the increased rate of frequency at which teachers are asked to cover other classes originally not in their schedule, can we really keep referring to this practice as *unexpected*? It has become normalized to assign additional classes to experienced teachers for subjects they know little or nothing about. Under these circumstances, teachers have learned how to mask their inadequate preparation to teach these subjects. Sometimes they seek support from colleagues familiar with the subject to give them a crash course about the fundamentals, or they study the textbook to consume enough information to give the appearance of possessing knowledge about the subject. It is a short-term and short-sighted strategy of survival intended to achieve the appearance of a credible performance.

This is not to suggest that last-minute random assignments to lead classes in unfamiliar subjects should ever be normalized. But having both a content specialist and an instructional specialist available to coach teachers who are on the receiving end of those random assignments might help maintain some level of stability during the transition phase. At a minimum, schools could assign substitutes for a week, during which time teachers assigned to take over on a full-time basis could consult with specialists to prepare lessons. In the initial weeks, a co-teaching model, where content and instructional specialists can take on co-teaching responsibilities, may be very helpful to support transitioning newly assigned teachers mid-year. Modeling practices while working with newly assigned teachers may help accelerate the process of nurturing and cultivating their professional skills to enhance their knowledge of content while building competency in planning and providing quality instruction.

We are witnessing the current plight of teachers' early departure from a profession they held the highest hopes of making their career. Providing direct school-based support to teachers is how we help them remain in classrooms. Too overwhelmed with managing the day-to-day routines, teachers don't even have the luxury of time to reflect on best practices. Expecting them to independently work additional hours after school or over the weekend to explore ways to expand their knowledge of content is an unreasonable *ask*. And even if they had the time, where would they go to refresh and further develop or expand their knowledge of content they are assigned?

New school years can begin with many surprises, including announcements, at the first district-wide meeting for all teachers and school leaders, about newly purchased education resources for each grade level. Educational companies given access to newly hired department leaders during the spring or summer are generally free to make purchasing decisions without a vetting system that includes input from knowledgeable and experienced veteran teachers. In school districts that see veteran teachers as essential to their decision-making process, teachers are given time to review and share their input regarding whether or not the assertions made by a company's representative are valid. Illustrations in education books are designed to be visually appealing. However, experienced teachers are quite savvy with determining whether or not educational products align key concepts and units with district and state standards. The degree of credibility claimed by company representatives needs verification from experienced teachers. Veteran teachers' judgment should be included when evaluating claims about ease of use for teachers, assignments tailored to each student's learning profile, inclusion of learning objectives embedded in rigorous lessons, and other features that distinguish quality resources from those unworthy of shelves in classrooms. However, teachers lack time—another valuable and overlooked resource—to explore and adequately determine degree of any education resource's suitability for class lessons. In addition to helping teachers explore and update content resources, professional content specialists can dedicate the time needed to cultivate best teaching practices. Bridging instructional gaps in classrooms will be made possible by the inclusion of qualified specialists skilled in expanding every teacher's knowledge of content.

CHAPTER 7

Instructional Support Specialist

A Personal Journey of Learning Deficiencies

BASED ON MY OWN PERSONAL LEARNING EXPERIENCES, IT'S difficult to say with absolute certainty that the availability of an instructional support specialist would have resolved my learning deficiencies. But it might have been beneficial to have teachers trained and able to share learning strategies with students to better prepare us for our educational journey. Looking back on my own educational journey from elementary school through my first year of college, I inherited learning deficiencies that then followed me from one level to the next, reflected in low or failing grades. But I also inherited sole responsibility for the poor grades I received, while also being convinced I alone had "earned" those grades.

Blaming students for simply revealing what they do not understand seems unfair. Teachers and professors not adequately trained in diverse methods of instruction and unaware of the need to teach students how to learn should bear some responsibility for student performance outcomes. Additional instructional time, when offered, was not always beneficial because it would likely have included the same instruction method I initially failed to understand. When teachers fail to recognize that a new method of instruction is needed, those sessions generally produce the same result. I, like so many other students, bore the burden of being held responsible for failing to understand. I am not trying to find fault or place blame with my former teachers for my learning deficiencies. I just think having educators trained to deliver quality instruction and expansion of their methods of instructional practices would have better served both teachers and students. Familiarity with student learning profiles and identifying compatible methods of instruction tailored to the learning needs of students, is what is needed. Instead, too many educators accept the standard practice of a one-dimensional instructional response, which ignores the need to individualize instruction. The one-dimensional response illustrates why instructional specialists would be beneficial in advancing instructional practices that will help teachers achieve high competency standards.

When a system permits reliance on outdated instructional practices, one does have to wonder if standardized assessments and other tests reflect how well students are adapting to instructional practices rather than fully comprehending content. Learning how to navigate one's way through each class by adapting or mimicking a teacher's method of instruction, generally by simply repeating back what was said or shown, does not demonstrate learning. But it is a survival strategy. Students who are actually given opportunities to overcome learning deficiencies not only will thrive but will be equipped to become lifelong learners.

Self-Taught Solutions to Advance My Education

The college courses I was able to enroll in and at least understand some modicum of information, enabled me to grab the first rung of a ladder. Sometimes I remained stationary and held on to that first rung for dear life. Over time, I applied myself, mostly due to sheer will and wanting to avoid failing, and I was able to do enough to earn a passing grade. Not knowing how to study, or what to highlight, due to my inability to differentiate between what was deemed essential and nonessential, caused me to go heavy on the highlighting process. Page after page of text was highlighted, followed by notations of entire paragraphs that should have been summarized. But having never learned how to write summaries, I deduced it was in my best interest to just include every word that was written. I never actually rewrote a book verbatim, but I did come close on a few occasions.

By my sophomore year, where I continued to struggle, I began the arduous process of teaching myself how to learn. At my school, there was no benefit to memorizing volumes of information and regurgitating back to the teacher. Most the assignments were in an open-question format. Responses had to include your perspective—I was totally clueless about what that word meant the first time I encountered it—reasons supported by evidence for your perspective, analysis of what authors meant by various phrases, or opinions of decisions made by the main character. English Literature classes began my transformation into an avid reader. The books and topics were interesting. I knew my school was liberal, but some of the books assigned were unbelievably bizarre, yet quite fascinating. There were also the classics about folks like Captain Ahab, who was notorious for making classic mistakes. My summation of that story included my thoughts about Ahab's decision to go in pursuit of a whale that was ten times larger than his wooden ship; I wrote that it was perilous and a bit unwise. Written along the margins of my essay were numerous reasons for my grade. The professor highlighted the absence of responses to questions about symbolisms, most notably, "What was the symbolism of Ahab's relationship with Moby Dick?" and "How did it impact his decision to persist in his pursuit of capturing this particular whale?" I was clueless.

Before enrolling in this course, I had never read the book, nor had I ever heard of the term *symbolism* prior to its appearance on the course syllabus. I was at a major disadvantage. I was rightfully called out for ignoring the directions that were made explicit. I finally understood that it was unacceptable to write responses to questions that did not include any reference to what was specifically asked. I had been hoping whatever I wrote would demonstrate to the professor that, while I may not have understood what the question meant, I had some understanding of the events that occurred. Apparently, though, regurgitating key events did not impress him. Thankfully he would not deviate from the standards and expectations he made clear. His job was not to teach me concepts college students were already expected to know, or at least have some familiarity with.

Realizing the standards and expectations of every professor were nonnegotiable, I had to choose between two options: I could choose to continue receiving barely passing and failing grades and accept what I felt in that moment: overwhelmed, with a deep sense of being too ill-equipped to ever complete college. Or I could wipe away my tears, quit feeling sorry for myself, and forge ahead down a different path. The second option was fueled by my strong sense of pride, and a dose of preferring to avoid feeling humiliated if I flunked out.

Once I decided quitting was not an option, I shed my comfort zone encased inside what felt like a bubble of fear and shifted to new study habits. Shedding my former comfort zone meant I was no longer a high school student in need of handholding and guidance. I was responsible for figuring out my learning deficiencies and overcoming them. It was definitely a "reset" moment. I discontinued my tendency to continue being casually dismissive, and instead developed a habit of admitting what I did not know and identifying the resources I needed to elevate my learning skills while concurrently strengthening my comprehension skills so I could become a more competent scholar.

During my period of transformation, I enrolled in English and American Literature courses because reading seemed to anchor me. Learning came more easily because, once I had learned how to read through a lens of curiosity, it gradually increased my appetite for reading. Eventually, I looked forward to encountering new words, concepts, and themes. My increased consumption of books improved my reading, vocabulary, and learning skills. No longer intimidated by any course syllabus, I continued my transformation in other ways. I went from a student who desired to be invisible in classes to a participant no longer afraid to raise my hand and ask questions in class. I was no longer concerned about feeling inadequate or embarrassed. However, I didn't contribute to discussions unless I had something I felt strongly about needing to say. I began to see the difference between those vying to get the attention of the professor and other students like me who are not invested in being eager to please or take up oxygen. Frankly, I occasionally became annoyed by the presence of my peers who spoke but added nothing of value and deprived others from having meaningful interactions. On paper, I had once been one of those who took up a lot of oxygen. I can't help wondering what professors experienced while attempting to correct my assignments prior to my transformation from inadequately prepared high school student to someone who really enjoyed growing into a thoughtful scholar.

Resetting my expectations motivated me to learn how to work my way from the bottom up. Gaining comfort in reading definitely spurred my growth in learning. Libraries that had initially scared and overwhelmed me became a valued resource at some point during my freshman year. Prior to college, I wasn't that familiar with who Dewey was, why he or she had a decimal system named after them, nor how the decimal system worked. That may have had to do with my only level of familiarity of the word "decimals" introduced, but not well understood, during math lessons. Perhaps a little spillover of my aversion to anything related to a subject I struggled with may have contributed to my apprehension of encountering that word again. In spite of *decimal* being used in a different context, it did not matter because the die of fear was already cast. It likely contributed to my lack of familiarity with how the library system worked. My appreciation for libraries and other resources I underutilized during college occasionally makes me reflect on how my education experience could have been enhanced if I had known then what I know now.

Learning Skills Essential for Learning Success

The value of lessons learned is the opportunity to be in a position to pass those lessons on to others. Throughout my leadership role in a high school, embedded in one of the poorest communities in the city and state, I wore many hats, including that of instructional leader. As a leader of an alternative school populated by students who just wanted to do enough to earn a high school diploma and then get on with their lives, I wondered, "Get on to where in your life?" Recognizing the limited opportunities for young adults opting to settle with just a high school diploma provided the opening I needed to attempt to change their minds. Introducing them to an array of other options, including attending college, was met with a lack of enthusiasm. Understandably, they were weary of remaining in school to continue with their education. Explaining the benefits of attending college did little to improve their level of interest, until a school assembly presentation showed the difference in employment and salary opportunities for young adults who earned high school diplomas compared with those who earned college degrees. That truly piqued their interest.

I was determined not to get on the bandwagon of encouraging students not in possession of the prerequisite college-readiness skills to apply to higher education programs, where many colleges and universities discovered the profitability of filling seats with students of color from urban communities. To have done so would have been reckless and negligent, considering what I had personally experienced as a student unprepared for college. Thankful for the lessons I was insufficiently prepared for but had to learn while attending college, I realized that unless my staff and I made significant changes to address gaps between our high school instructional practices, curriculum offerings, and academic expectations, we would be setting up our students for failure. Of equal importance was the need to help students develop specific college-level learning skills. If they were to succeed in college, they needed to arrive equipped with learning strategies that would enable them to perform a range of tasks.

All subjects were designed to include lessons using research projects to strengthen learned strategies. Assignments were embedded with tasks requiring in-depth reading of a variety of content, analysis, note-taking, essay organization, descriptive language use, the distinguishing of facts from opinions, citation and accurate referencing of sources, summarizing, and oratory presentations. My college experience fueled my desire to ensure our students were prepared to successfully navigate their way through a two- or four-year college program.

Bridging the gap between high school and college was so important, it led to the creation of our College Prep Academy for all seniors. The program was supported through partnerships with several college professors who welcomed our students in their classes each semester. One of our partnerships with a dean of undergraduate students led to invitations to campus events, including scavenger hunts and co-sponsoring an annual conference for our high school faculty and college professors. Collaborative opportunities benefited members of both faculties committed to identifying skills needed to bridge gaps from high school to college and support a successful transition into and through college. The conferences revealed some common challenges that professors and high school teachers encountered when inheriting students who arrive with learning deficiencies. Those conferences also confirmed we were on the right track. Merging instruction of content with the development of learning skills is essential to learning success.

Contemporary Practices in Today's Lesson Plans

Investing time in developing, expanding, and deepening a teacher's knowledge of the content and subjects they teach is helpful, but it is no guarantee of their ability to effectively instruct others about what they know. Knowledge of content is completely different from knowing how to teach, yet they are treated as though one seamlessly interlocks with the other. If there is no understanding of the need to separate knowledge of content from the ability to effectively teach, a teacher's competency in both areas is greatly compromised.

Now that we understand the practice of conflating content with ability to teach, let's consider the consequences of teachers endowed with one but not the other. One consequence is the disservice to students who are assigned teachers knowledgeable about subjects, but possessing inadequate instructional skills. In fact, depriving teachers of instructional development support impacts their ability to teach what they know if they lack an understanding of how to teach, regardless of what they know.

There is universal agreement within every community about the overarching mission of schools. The mission is to advance every student's educational progression. To achieve that, students must obtain mastery of content. However, attaining skills at barely passing levels is not an acceptable option. In fact, when teachers don't know how to teach, it impacts students' ability to learn. When students make a sincere effort to grasp but are unable to understand what is being taught, they equate learning with frustration. One possible strategy to prevent students from experiencing further frustration would be for teachers to examine alternative methods of instruction.

Merging Cultural Identity with Instruction

Hip Hop is currently among instructional alternatives emerging to the forefront of new pedagogical models designed to engage student interest in learning. Hip Hop Pedagogy merges content with culturally relevant areas of genuine interest to students to elevate critical thinking, literacy, and other skills across all content areas. This is referred to by some as Culturally Responsive Pedagogy (CRP). Educational pioneers like LaMar Queen, Christopher Emdin, Edmund Adjapong, Nolan Jones, Terrance Sims, A. D. Carson, and others have shared innovative ways to strengthen and sustain student engagement in learning. The various models represent how the pioneers of contemporary education reimagined ways to take traditional curriculum for all subjects and reframe instruction to be inclusive of urban students' social, ethnic, and musical interests in ways those elements influence their cultural identity. The cornerstones of Hip Hop's success go beyond influencing musical culture. Its artistry is a historical treasure trove of storytelling that elevates cultural awareness about inequities and a range of conditions that have deprived people of color from accessing equitable social and economic gains related to freedoms, voting rights, quality education, freedom from profiling, and protection from overzealous extreme law enforcement. CRP focuses on bridging curriculum with each student's perspective and personal life experiences to strengthen their educational experiences.

CRP and Hip Hop in urban schools is resonating with students because learning happens through a unique and dynamic process. The instructional paradigm is an ethnic-studies curriculum centered around the cultural identity of the students. In some instances, students are the primary contributors to lessons, where their perspectives, interests, and ideas influence how lessons are taught. Their input about social issues, personal aspirations, and pride and concerns about communities they reside in are given a meaningful presence in classrooms. One example of evidence of what matters to students being valued is how lessons taught are embedded in musical beats, rhymes, and other familiar elements of Hip Hop music, make learning fun and memorable. Instruction of content and the process of learning is made more personal.

As students ascend to higher grade levels, instruction scaffolds up, integrating more rigorous levels of learning to strengthen every student's education, but CRP practices prevent more rigorous assignments from intimidating students. Courses that used to be regarded as too difficult, such as STEM (Science, Technology, Engineering, and Math) have been made relatable. When students' culture is represented in curriculum, lessons, and assignments, they are more apt to embrace what they experience. Students find purpose in their education when it is delivered through innovative and culturally relevant models. Whereas Hip Hop was once shunned and criticized, its musical influence has elevated to one of America's popular genres. Evidence of the enormous heights reached by artists of rap, spoken word, and other media platforms represented across the broad spectrum of Hip Hop occurred in 2021 when November was officially designated Hip Hop Month. While such educational pioneers as Queen, Emdin, Adjapong, Jones, Sims, Carson, and others have been at the forefront of successfully merging Hip Hop with education, Flocabulary's online learning platform and other forms of institutionalizing culture with education are innovations that are being embraced in a cross-section of classes representing students across all ethnicities.

Instructional Support Specialists Can Solve Jigsaw Puzzle: Aligning Standards with Lessons

If no intervention occurs, then, over time, students who are experiencing ongoing educational frustration become fatigued. Evidence of growing educational frustration and fatigue can be seen in incomplete assignments submitted or in a refusal to turn in any work. When that occurs, students are aware that their decision to stop making an effort to learn will earn them a failing grade.

Exploration of advances in all content areas is time consuming. Another obstacle is having no time available to explore those advances or to research advanced models and methods of instruction of contemporary content. Rarely do teachers find the time needed to determine how to align methods of instruction of updated content with each student's learning profile. Why? Teachers lack the time needed to explore. But exploration without professional and knowledgeable guidance could result in pursuing ideas and purchasing products unworthy of any classroom if the promised outcomes aren't produced. Experienced content and instructional support specialists possess the qualifications needed to work with teachers to research and verify credibility of resources.

Relying on new teachers to know how to link standards with instruction is cause for concern—not because they cannot eventually learn to link standards with instruction, but because it takes time, practice, and guidance to ensure it is done correctly. While the standards for skills targeted for development may be clearly enunciated, the cross-referencing process of linking the standards to learning planned in lessons may not be mutually aligned. It's equivalent to trying to assemble pieces in jigsaw puzzle without the benefit of an image to show what the puzzle should look like upon completion. Then there is the risk of not fully comprehending what the standards mean. Evidence of gaps between standards and planned instruction are most likely to be found in some teachers' lesson plan books.

In fairness to all teachers, some highly effective instructional methods can take a few years to perfect. Expiration dates may not apply to models that have produced high rates of success. But in fairness to students, some updated assessment to verify the validity of past and current instructional methods is needed to prevent the recurrent use of outdated practices that have not produced performance outcomes at the highest standard. Even best practices maintained over a span of years warrant review prior to entering a teacher's lesson plans.

There are other obstacles that make replacing dated lesson plans a challenge. Teachers are understandably weary of new methods and models promoted, in some cases, almost annually in their district, but particularly when a rotation from one superintendent to another occurs. School districts enduring cycles of people being rotated in and then out of positions from the superintendent to department heads and other administrative leaders generally have learned to expect changes in curriculum, pedagogical practices, school management, and operation policies. While those changes are intended to improve areas that *the data* show need immediate attention, how those expectations for transitions are communicated and released as non-negotiable mandates, with little to no proof of their efficacy, often contributes to lack of enthusiasm to embrace those changes. For many veteran teachers who have heard it all before, it tends to make them tighten their grip on curriculum and instructional practices that have, from their perspective, proven quite reliable. Resistance is a response to the whiplash effect of pendulum swings from one leadership style to an entirely different one when, within a few years, those thought to be competent leaders demonstrate they are unsuited for the position.

Another contributing obstacle is an objective assessment of the status of resources currently used in schools. What is their condition? Date of purchase is also important. Is the content relevant, or does it contain outdated information? Have resources undergone an assessment to identify whether or not the content presented aligns with current academic standards? Inventories are needed for all educational resources to determine degree of efficacy. Efficacy of academic performance outcomes can be determined by use of uniform and consistent assessments capable of capturing accurate data. Since standards across all subjects are evolving, former assessments may lack sufficient representation of updated skills targeted for development. Even those assessments perceived as highly reliable occasionally need to be replaced. Ironically these days, electronic devices, like smart phones, purchased just last year may already be deemed obsolete; yet the lengthy shelf life of textbooks is quite mysterious.

All teachers, whether veteran or those in their first year, would benefit from the expertise of professionals, knowledgeable about planning and teaching lessons. More importantly, instruction is not isolated to planning for and teaching to homogeneous student populations. The presence of diverse learners performing at different levels and possessing different learning styles and profiles makes planning and delivering instruction highly complex. Teachers are likely to start with a written lesson planned for their class, but the broad range of learners present in every classroom requires the expertise of a professional familiar with diverse methods of instruction. It is imperative for teachers to identify and become familiar with instructional practices that engage every student in learning.

Demystifying Standards to Allow Transparency for Students

Instruction specialists can also work with teachers to teach students the meaning of standards embedded in rubric, district, state, and national assessments. Transforming the meaning of each standard into *student-friendly* language will help students become familiar with tools used to assess their performance levels. Helping students take ownership of standards can convert fear of the unknown to full transparency, simply by demystifying standards. After standards are revealed, they can be integrated into lesson plans as learning objectives students can aspire to achieve. Standards translated into *student-speak,* to allow them to grasp exactly what is meant, should be embedded in lessons across all content areas. Why must standards, that determine level of achievement, be a mystery to those whose performance levels will be judged?

The next concern has to be conveyed gently. Teachers using outdated lesson plans, content, and pedagogical practices not aligned with the learning profiles of current student populations is another reason for assessing teacher competency. Any attempt to move veteran teachers from their comfort zones, reflected in the continued use of years-old lesson plans, is the responsibility of school leaders. However, leaving that responsibility solely in the hands of newly assigned school leaders who inherit veteran staff is a bit of a quagmire. There's no joy in asking veteran teachers to "kindly relinquish your lesson plan book," if you have not had a chance to demonstrate leadership skills in curriculum development and instruction. Teachers need to see evidence that those in superior positions possess superior skills in areas they are going to scrutinize and to which they are going to suggest improvements. Professional specialists qualified in instructional planning of lessons will actually free school leaders, responsible for managing schools, to wear fewer hats and become more competent in carrying out their duties as school leader.

Why We Should Refrain from Predetermining Students' Levels of Ability

When teachers consider ways to make classrooms more inclusive of all students, they find that managing the broad range of learning styles, learning profiles, and different levels of performance is one of their most challenging responsibilities. You may have noticed there is no reference to the term *performance level of ability.* Terms like *level of ability* presume students are locked into a predetermined level of learning ability, which is a biased assumption made about their ability to learn at higher levels. Without the benefit of instruction aligned with each student's learning profile, that (a) may result in significant performance improvements and (b) demonstrate the true levels of ability they are capable of achieving throughout their 13 years of education, we should refrain from our tendency to preordain students to learning expectations that are based solely on what their *current level of ability* is, and not on what could be their actual potential growth in ability.

To predetermine one's level of ability without distinguishing it from their future potential level of ability is how our education tracking system occurred. Levels of ability were used to justify and make permanent the segregation of students into learning groups. The tracking system did not coincidentally assign overwhelming populations of students of color, who were routinely perceived as meeting the qualifications of the lowest level of performers, particularly in integrated school districts, in slow-learner classes. It was intentional. Sadly, despite advancements in education reforms over several decades, the tracking system thrived. In many cases, students showing little to no improvement were then referred for an evaluation where they were found to have "special needs" and were placed in special education classes. The ability to apply a different name to any process or practice that mimics its predecessor, such as tracking, may give the appearance of its being new. Often former practices, disguised behind new names, are continued because we have not come up with a better and more effective system, despite the span of decades in which annual national tests showed, in this case, that tracking resulted in little if any progress. In a majority of schools, once placed in the lowest performing group, students were locked into lower performing groups at each subsequent grade level. There is no greater proof of the consequences of branding someone a below-level performer, permanently and unfairly tethering them to the same status throughout the rest of their journey in public education.

Student Learning Profiles Should Determine Instructional Resources

While one alternative to tracking, which groups students based on current level of ability, is to diversify instruction, *how* to achieve diversification of instruction is the real conundrum. Instructional support specialists could assist teachers in identifying learning resources by first acquainting teachers with the learning profile of each of their students. Student learning profiles generally refer to how students learn best, including what their individual learning preferences are. Assessing learning profiles that are so broadly defined can be a daunting task for any teacher. The addition of professional development specialists knowledgeable about content, instruction, and behavior management would be beneficial in determining what forms of learning profile assessments would be helpful and under what circumstances. In some cases, learning profiles may have to be content-specific to determine compatible methods of instruction. Then there are other students who are easily socially distracted, or who are highly distracting to others during lessons that consume so much instructional time when teachers have to constantly stop to redirect them back on task. Assessing learning profiles cannot be limited to improving academic performances. If behaviors interfere with learning, then a priority must be placed on to how to approach and reverse attention-getting behaviors that impede learning. But if the disruption or behavioral distractions tend to occur in only one or a few, but not all classes, then addressing the learning gaps revealed in the student's learning profile assessment may show a link between attention-getting behaviors exhibited as a potential manifestation of the student's academic frustration.

Pedagogical performances in classrooms will be greatly improved by having an instructional support specialist consult with teachers to learn about various models for planning lessons. Whether models are designed for whole class instruction, small-cluster learning groups, or independent learning tasks, all three have an element in common: each model must be linked to learning objectives, academic standards, and student learning profiles. Lesson planning is essential to cultivating exceptional classrooms. It is, however, the initial step of a multilevel teaching process. Discovering *how to* engage and sustain student engagement in learning relies on method and delivery of instruction as well as many other factors. The list of responsibilities expected of instructional specialists is immense, but it may help readers recognize and appreciate the enormity of responsibilities teachers are expected to perform to meet the highest standards. The degree to which any teacher is expected to effectively perform each responsibility at the highest level, while also taking responsibility for the social and emotional well-being of each student, makes the demands of their teaching time astronomically more challenging. While some manage those responsibilities, many more struggle. Those who struggle ought to be entitled access to resources to improve their quality of instruction and classroom management skills. Each specialist, working in partnership with teachers and, when needed, collaboratively with other specialists, will accelerate the professional growth of all teachers and other staff members.

For more about the roles and responsibilities of the instructional support specialist, see page 179 in the appendix.

CHAPTER 8

Differentiating Technology Maintenance from Computer Literacy Instruction

IF A SIGNIFICANT VOLUME OF CURRENTLY AVAILABLE YET UNFILLED positions exist within the technology sector across many industries, isn't that an indication of the lack of educational preparation contributing to employment gaps? Employment opportunities are evident in the number of job postings advertising a need for skilled technology employees at various-level positions. Yet our public education system in many communities has not made sufficient investment in computers, computer science, and literacy courses needed to prepare students for current and future employment opportunities in the era of a technology revolution. Some schools do not even have the most basic technology resources, including fully funded technology support positions occupied by experts capable of managing the overall maintenance of the school's entire computer network and technology system. A nationwide inventory of current technology resources in every public school would probably show the level of disparity between high-income communities, with highly skilled technology support specialists to oversee all matters related to the digital needs and operation of all electronic devices, and schools at the lower end of the economic spectrum, which typically lack those same resources. In addition to having highly skilled technology support specialists, economically well-off communities also have additional technology staffing positions available to teach computer science courses.

The investment in the technology assets in communities that have made technology and computer science a priority has produced well-educated and technology-skilled students prepared for the workforce that their counterparts in low-income communities have been unprepared for—until now. We know what the recipe for success is. We have decades of evidence showing the benefits of investing in technology resources and computer science education. It is time for our public education system to close the technology gaps in all schools. Mirroring the priorities of socio-economically well-off communities, our federal government can use the same roadmap of policy and financial investment in schools that lack those resources, to replicate the same high level of college and career success in and beyond the tech industry, which so desperately needs well-educated and highly skilled tech applicants.

Consequences of Inadequate Computer Science Education

Once the COVID pandemic forced schools to transition from in-person instruction to remote learning, a few major impediments obstructed the transition process. Insufficient laptops, lack of teacher and student familiarity with instructional models on digital platforms, and numerous gaps in computer science education proved a major hindrance to schools' making a successful transition. In many public schools there were insufficient quantities of computers. But in schools that had sufficient numbers of computers, an embarrassing number of students were unfamiliar with how to use them. *That was an alarming revelation!*

It took a health pandemic to force all schools to recognize the extreme digital divide between availability of resources and knowledge of how to use them. The sudden disappearance of in-person learning showed how much our entire education system relied on traditional instructional models. Little attention or funding was given to technology until remote learning forced everyone to appreciate its value as the primary way to ensure the continuation of every student's education. Returning to in-person instruction can no longer permit casual indifference or minimization of the role of technology in all classrooms. Use of electronic devices and access to instructional models across a variety of digital platforms catapulted to higher status on the lists of priorities across every school district. Schools need funding to hire computer experts trained in maintaining the operation of digital devices and networks. But the health pandemic made it even more evident that every school also needs a computer science specialist to train and elevate teacher competency with digital resources.

The custodial care of electronic devices and ensuring everything operates at maximum capacity will never stop being a priority. Yet, in many schools there are still no full-time tech positions. Imagine the constraints of having to function without the expertise of a tech specialist, capable of overseeing the digital operation and maintenance of the school's entire arsenal of technology resources. Lacking both the digital resources and tech experts to maintain operation of electronic devices puts a strain on opportunities to enrich learning. The range of educational learning platforms is expanding, but with no experts available to link an entire network of electronic devices that support each school's capacity to provide and support access to technology resources, students are deprived opportunities to experience a 21st century education. The platforms needed to support hybrid and remote instruction located in designated alternative learning spaces require reliable technology resources, fully scaled-up to meet the demands of our current century's expansive educational resources.

Hybrid and remote instruction rely on every technology resource to have the capacity to work where and when needed. Given how the COVID pandemic unmasked the deep fault lines in education gaps among low-income families unable to purchase the proper equipment and internet connection for their home, city officials should invest in providing bandwidth and digital devices in municipal and community-based organizations in every neighborhood. One step in remedying fault lines would be to provide a map identifying the address and location of every digital and operationally ready resource for remote learning service to all residents in neighborhoods without access to internet in their homes. Ideally, cities, towns, and businesses should work with technology companies to install, for every residence, internet access required for remote learning as well as accommodating parents needing to work from home. The new and highly preferred model of working from home is an option exercised by many in the labor force across the country. While an unintended benefit introduced in response to the COVID pandemic, it is another clear example of our broadening digital landscape and why students need to be educated about the tools and devices that make working in other locations possible or necessary.

Making the Case for a Technology Curriculum and Instruction Specialist

As schools were preparing for transitioning education to homes for remote learning, districts that had laptops and other devices available did their best to distribute them to students. Despite availability of laptops for every student, it came as a surprise that large numbers of students were illiterate in computer science, beyond the rudimentary operations of a digital device. In addition to lacking basic computer science skills, schools that did not have sufficient funds for courses to develop skills in coding, programming, digital fluency, and information literacy further disadvantaged already educationally disadvantaged students. Access to learning platforms, including how to log into live-streamed lessons on Zoom, was nearly impossible. As frustrations mounted, remote-learning sessions saw a significant drop in student participation. It was a catastrophe that could have been avoided if only students had been able to participate in computer science classes during in-person learning. We now know with certainty how the absence of computer science curriculum and instruction prevented students from continuing their education. We also know it was also not the solution to expect classroom teachers to step in to facilitate instruction in any area they were unfamiliar with and had no training in. Yet, it was what districts decided was the solution in several schools. Schools would not hire uncertified and fully licensed teachers to instruct math without proof of their having met the minimum qualifications, but they had no problem with assigning them responsibility for teaching computer skills. Most teachers were not even provided a basic manual, or anything resembling a *Beginners Course for How to Use Computers*. But even among those who were, do we really think that was a sufficient level of education?

As obvious as it sounds, it must be said out loud: when communities lack adequate technology education, it's due to the insufficient or total absence of any instruction related to technology. It's not widely known, but often computers in schools of low-income neighborhoods are secondhand devices donated, and are a one-time act of generosity by businesses needing to replace their equipment. Being a recipient of second or third generations of working computers is often the only means of accessing technology resources. Ironically, schools inherit outdated but useable electronic equipment from business organizations because of the businesses' need to invest in technology upgrades to retain their competitive edge. Schools that had no computers greatly appreciated those donations. A common practice among businesses is periodically increasing investments for digital upgrades. The digital upgrades made across every industry support their businesses in meeting new demands. Technical upgrades are the lifeblood of companies needing to remain in existence. They are committed to keeping or surpassing the pace of their competitors by making continual advancements in technology. Many companies try to anticipate future trends, and they offer training courses to employees to advance their skills to help the company stay ahead of their competitors. Unfortunately, that same aspirational model of advancing along the technology learning curve is not a priority of our public education system.

Being repositories of secondhand technology resources in schools located in disenfranchised neighborhoods shows that education is not viewed as a priority. Schools left to rely on outdated computers donated years ago now have closets filled with equipment that is either barely functioning or broken. But the problem is not just broken computers in need of repair. Until we take a page from corporations that understand the need to make technology a priority, students graduating from high school with technology-skill deficiencies will remain at a disadvantage. Right now, they lack the digital and computer literacy skills needed to apply for the most basic entry-level employment positions in technology positions currently available. This is just one example of our education system's being underutilized in ways that could benefit students. Adding insult to injury, schools without adequate funds are forced to rely on the distribution of beginner's course manuals to teachers not properly trained to teach the content. When teachers are not properly trained to teach any subject, it negatively influences the level of interest in using manuals. Manuals are no substitute for in-person training by experts. For many years, veteran teachers have managed to successfully cultivate instructional practices without technology resources. Integrating technology resources without professional training and adequate time to ramp-up use on a regular basis is why in many of those classes' use of technology remains dormant. The digital evolution inside of schools was delayed for many reasons. Some may wish to accuse school staff of being tech-phobic and resisting the advent of technology in classrooms. But delayed integration of technology in classrooms was due to the absence of professional development training—ongoing guidance throughout the school year—so teachers were left to figure it out on their own.

Until computer science resources—digital devices and networks—were installed, it was impossible to merge content across multiple digital-educational platforms to enrich students' educational experiences. Quality technology resources used to promote quality instructional models across diverse platforms enrich a student's educational experience by strengthening learning retention. Retaining what is learned improves memorization of content. Memorization of content leads to confidence, which increases a willingness to further independently explore. Frequent use of computers is similar to learning a foreign language. One must be given opportunities to apply a new language learned by constantly generalizing its use inside and outside of the classroom. Application through generalization on a regular basis makes users more comfortable. That process also incentivizes further use of the language, or in this case computer skills, independently as one's comfort level increases. High school students eager to travel to France after taking French classes are generally enthusiastic about traveling to French-speaking regions to explore the customs and cultures because they have been well prepared and feel comfortable speaking the language.

The same principle applies to limited access to computer courses in classrooms and expecting untrained teachers to provide instruction or inspire independent learning. Schools that do not provide students access to computer science courses and instruction negatively impact their ability to access future opportunities, including succeeding in college or being eligible to apply for tech-based employment. Being ineligible does not always disqualify potential candidates for employment. Some companies are in such dire need, they hire based on conditions, including participation in training programs where trainees are required to meet specific standards before being officially hired. Candidates who do not achieve the standards may unfairly be judged as incapable. But in fairness to them, without adequate training and time to familiarize themselves, it is equivalent to placing students in a foreign country without the ability to speak or understand the language. Had they had the benefit of being educated and then had opportunities to apply skills learned to strengthen their competence, which in turn would have elevated their confidence, they would have likely been eligible for the job.

Evolution of Digital Footprints in and Beyond Schools

In schools with fully upgraded technology resources operating at high capacity across digital networks that enable connectivity in every classroom, there are no sign-up lists posted outside of computer labs. Classrooms equipped with all of the latest technology have had the benefit of creating lessons that engage students in learning using a myriad of educational platforms. Research projects that result in creative and artistically aesthetic infographics and other digitally produced work have been made possible by expanding every student's and teacher's arsenal of technology devices and comfort in operating them, by way of curriculum and instruction from qualified technology instructors. Coding courses, program development, and creation of self-made games and videos are second nature.

But another distinct advantage for students whose teachers receive continual instruction from trained technology instructors, is access to the abundance of future employment opportunities, where companies place a premium on prospective candidates who are digitally fluent. There is a demand for employees skilled in analysis and capable of artistically transferring analytics into visually accessible content. Many companies are interested in hiring creative project designers. Highly skilled and computer-literate project designers are given freedoms to openly create new platforms for companies interested in expanding their brand to reach broader markets. STEM (Science, Technology, Math, Engineering) programs have become very popular and are in high demand because of the increased rate of employment opportunities for highly qualified and skilled students who are trained in computer science.

In summary, advancement in technology requires maintenance to ensure all equipment is fully operational at all times and experts are available to train teachers in the variety of ways technology resources can be used to enhance instruction across all content areas. But technology is also the lifeline of our education system under a range of circumstances that enable students to continue receiving their education. To ensure that education continues to be accessible to all students at all times, we must follow a complex series of steps; but, at a minimum, we can achieve a greater degree of success throughout the transition phase by instituting the following technology-preparedness practices during in-person learning time:

- Upgrade the tech network; make sure all satellite classroom spaces are fully equipped with tech resources. (*See Satellite Classroom Networks, starting on page 152.*)
- Schedule instruction on learning platforms during in-person learning to acclimate students.
- Embed into weekly class schedules all live-stream instructional platforms planned for remote learning, to familiarize students with resources.
- Provide technology orientation for teachers, students, and parents.

CHAPTER 9

Classroom Management Specialist

An Overview

Historically, high teacher turnover rates are most frequently due to discipline issues. Because every school is contending with a variety of discipline issues, it has become clear that every school needs a full-time classroom management specialist. Generally viewed as the most difficult areas schools need help addressing are issues related to bullying, as well as confrontations among students and their peers or students and staff. Truthfully, many schools may strongly desire more than one classroom management specialist. That's understandable, but it may not be necessary because successfully managed classrooms are the hallmark of well-planned quality instruction.

I have seen firsthand evidence of how instruction impacts the routine operation of a class. Engaging all students in learning is, in fact, one of the most effective classroom management tools many successful teachers rely on most among the items in their tool kit. How those teachers prepared the conditions in their classrooms for engagement in learning is really no mystery: they instituted classroom cultural norms. Having cultural norms established at the start of the school year achieved two very essential *must haves* for every classroom. The first *must have* in every classroom is to provide students with a clear understanding about expectations relating to conduct that contributes to a culture of safety, respect, and behaviors that make every member of the class feel welcome. The second *must have* is class routines.

Greater emphasis and supports are needed to help first-year teachers develop and implement whole-class management of routines so teachers will become more self-reliant in addressing disruptive behaviors and reducing dependency on school administrators. First-year and veteran teachers can find it infuriating, when a request for administrative assistance results in the only response being a student's temporary removal and assignment to a seat outside of the principal's office, after which they are sent back to the class with no sign of having been held accountable for whatever rule infraction occurred. And it may be an indication that the school administrators may actually be incapable of providing any effective advice or strategies to assist your efforts with holding students accountable.

It is possible to overcome the challenge of preventing classrooms from devolving into a chaotic environment, where most of a teacher's time is devoted to managing what feels more like an emergency room. Having a classroom management specialist knowledgeable about effective strategies can transform classrooms from one form of ER (emergency rooms) into highly productive *educational resource* (ER) environments. Students focus better when they can experience learning in a calm, safe, and well-organized classroom.

Whatever classroom management system or process is used, few teachers are familiar with ways to help students self-regulate their behaviors. Behaviorally, too many students seem to need external cues, in the form of policies, to guide their actions. All students need clearly stated expectations, but some require more explicit behavior standards. A classroom management specialist can create and support the implementation of various models or techniques needed to improve self-monitoring of behaviors. Students tend to respond to various forms of immediate feedback. It may be necessary to develop a reporting system that allows for instant gratification through direct feedback at the end of each academic period. Gradually, students can be weaned from micromanagement of behaviors at the end of each period to delaying their need for good and gratifying reports about their behavioral achievements to the end of each day. Strengthening their ability to self-monitor their behaviors is an effective method of turning responsibility for their decisions over to the students themselves. It not only reduces behaviors that disrupt lessons, but students appreciate recognition of positive changes in their behaviors.

It is important to use a fair process that includes behavior performance standards all students can achieve. In addition to behavior performance reports to assist those students needing more frequent and immediate feedback, some may also require more time to adjust to classroom performance expectations and standards. Similar to the diverse levels of performance across all academic subjects, students also adjust to classroom norms at a different pace. Some students may require different methods of instruction or more time and repetition to master academic skills. So too is the case among a population of students developing an understanding of classroom norms and then successfully meeting performance standards aligned with those norms. In any homogeneous population of students, being the same age in the same grade does not mean they arrive with the same emotional, social, psychological, physical, and academic learning profiles. In an ideal world, despite the broad range of diverse personalities that possess differing attitudes about compliance and conforming to rules, influenced by previous and sometimes complicated experiences with adults at school or home, every student would arrive ready to be compliant. Although students ages 11 and 12 in a classroom of 20 or more students are often perceived as having a lot in common with one another, their emotional, social, and behavioral development is as diverse as their individual personalities.

At this very moment, every school district has teachers in need of assistance developing their classroom management skills. In fact, given the impact of how disruptive behaviors often hinder teachers from teaching, it is evident that our public education system has to set a higher priority on helping teachers develop competency in managing their classes. To do that requires them to have access to resources that provide strategies designed to improve the conditions they are contending with in their classrooms each day.

Students Want to Know What Goals to Aspire to Achieve and How to Achieve Them

Providing transparency and clarity to all students about the *what, when, where, how,* and *why* of expectations reveals what is needed of them. If students are well informed about what they should aspire to achieve, then revealing achievable expectations generally helps elevate the willingness of most students to cooperate. Another useful strategy for encouraging cooperation is, while explaining the *do's* and *don'ts* related to behavior expectations, to place greater emphasis on the *do's*. The *do's* reveal what students can and should aspire to achieve.

As is often the case, one or more students may need additional time and attention to support their gradual transformation. Resistance to cooperation is a common strategy of attention-seeking students. Students who crave and engage in disruptive behaviors may be conditioned to welcome any form of attention, as long as the focus remains on them. The challenge of disengaging students from becoming a high-maintenance problem has no single remedy. Getting at the root cause takes time and a lot of patience. Deciding to ignore it is often recommended. But continuous blatant disregard for policies, rules, and the right of others to learn is unacceptable.

If teachers have not been trained to prevent or intervene, the disruptions to lessons will continue. Many veteran teachers have learned a tactic in which, within the first few days of school, they openly acknowledge some students' efforts of cooperation; this generally catches the attention of other students, who then follow the lead of peers acknowledged for doing what is expected. Efforts of cooperation may vary, but even the smallest sign of making an effort is worthy of acknowledgment. So often, pridefulness of not wanting to be *seen* wanting the teacher's positive attention, yet still truly wanting it, calls for finding subtle forms of acknowledgment and appreciation in those instances.

Possessing emotional intelligence is an important attribute and valuable asset. And it can be developed. Emotional intelligence enables teachers to refrain from taking behaviors personally. Whenever possible, teachers should respond to behaviors with a calm and neutral demeanor—even to the extent of pretending to wear an invisible layer of Teflon so nothing sticks. That comes in handy while teachers work on conditioning students to enjoy being recognized for good behavior. Teachers who freely and frequently engage in distributing appreciation can be the most influential agents of change in a student's behavior. Acts of appreciation are very effective. They also come in many different forms, including nonverbal communication by way of a warm smile or nod of approval directed at students when they do something that warrants recognizing.

Positive recognition often reinforces behaviors that then beget more good behavior. Receiving signals from teachers that communicate, "I see you and appreciate your effort. Keep up the great work," is quite gratifying to most students. If moments arise when students need reminders of behaviors in the *don't* category or redirecting their attention back onto tasks, stick with the nonverbal communication strategy to avoid calling out and openly admonishing students in the presence of their peers. Chances are those students know when they are stepping out of line because they tend to look at their teacher and either dare or expect their teacher to put them in check. If you possess a sense of humor, likening those moments to either a chess match or some version of Game of Thrones, may be useful and worth a chuckle. But in all seriousness, preventing any student's attempt to dethrone the teacher from the leadership role is a real thing in some—maybe many—classrooms. If a student succeeds in at least conveying the perception among his or her peers of occupying the proverbial throne, then the teacher's credibility as being in charge is greatly diminished; and credibility lost is very difficult to regain.

It's extremely difficult but necessary to hold all students accountable. However, many teachers need to be professionally trained in ways to hold students accountable in a manner that allows students to retain their dignity. Teachers who successfully channel a student's focus back on their work or calmly send them a look that communicates, "Come on, you can do better than that," instead of anger and disapproval, can and should share their success strategies with every colleague scheduled to work with the student throughout the day. That sharing can include whatever form of nonverbal and nonjudgmental communication strategies, tailored to whatever technique of communication, works best for individual students, particularly students with special needs.

Strategies that work in one class can be shared among the entire staff. This may encourage buy-in from colleagues, who could make a collective effort to see every student's potential and address mistakes as learning moments. Those who do buy-in and experience success resulting from tactics shared by colleagues could potentially see the quickest turnaround time of student behaviors, from inappropriate to appropriate. Pragmatically, though, school staff will need access to resources related to prevention, intervention, and the aftermath of incidents that unexpectedly or even expectedly spill over into a crisis. The important thing is to expect and then have a well-thought-out and explicit plan ready to deploy at the intervention stage. Then go one step further and map out a response plan capable of responsiveness beyond the intervention level.

Professional development for managing the range of potential circumstances has a greater chance of being successful when made available prior to the start of each school year and throughout the year. When school staff has an opportunity to learn de-escalation strategies prior to incidents' occurring, their sense of being able to handle whatever may come is heightened and gives them confidence. It can also have a calming effect. In addition to individual preparation, when an entire staff is well prepared in advance of potentially confrontational incidents, it can strengthen camaraderie and serve to unite everyone. Uniting everyone around intervention protocols for minimal to extreme circumstances promotes assurance about the collective presence and everyone knowing what to do. Safety nets are created when every adult on site makes him or herself available to support colleagues whenever a need arises for additional assistance to resolve conflicts. Classroom management specialists are needed to train staff about the various methods from how to be present without direct engagement to gradual levels of engagement in support of everyone's safety. Familiarity with non-intervention and intervention protocols reduces everyone's fear of getting involved. It's particularly important to be present at the early stages.

Teachers and entire school staff are desperately in need of professional support to prepare them for any circumstance. Of particular importance is their need to learn about the impact of how they communicate with students, physically and verbally, and the potential of both defusing or escalating incidents. Why am I harping on extinguishing potential fires that can be put out while small? It's because for many new teachers, lacking preparedness training puts them in untenable situations. We should all wonder what most often precedes a new teacher's decision to leave school one day and refuse to return. Usually, it is one of two circumstances: either behavior disruptions that rapidly escalate from minor incidents to raging firestorms in what feels like nanoseconds; and not knowing how to respond. Both are terrifying.

Just being aware of ways to refrain from meeting angry students at their level of frustration is an effective de-escalation strategy. It can be a game-changer to decide not to succumb to yelling but instead deliberately choose to remain calm while looking directly at the student and, in the most nonthreatening tone of voice, reassure them you want to hear their concerns; but if they want to be heard, they'll need to lower the volume and calmly explain what is going on. Teachers maintaining a calm and respectful demeanor while defusing a potential crisis prevents adding accelerant to an already inflammatory situation. Not fearing students when they are on the verge, or already in the process, of spiraling out of control requires mental and emotional restraint. Teachers should not inject themselves into the problem by taking a student's behavior personally; this almost always escalates their anger or aggressiveness.

During episodic moments at my school, the cavalry, which consisted of another staff member and me, required a quick assessment of the situation to determine how to mitigate or at least contain the problem to prevent it from blossoming into an even bigger problem. Outbursts were expected, but even our being prepared did not make them any less messy. Whatever we inherited, we always started the intervention process by giving our students the space, of our choosing, to explain their reasons for being upset. When it became possible to speak, it often surprised students when I informed them that they may have had a legitimate reason to be upset, but the manner in which they chose to express their displeasure overshadowed what might have been a justified grievance. If a student responds with, "Wait . . . what?" Their expression of perplexity is because they had not expected to hear what they just heard—and from their school leader, of all people. For students, it was rare to have someone in a position of authority actually care enough to want to hear their perspective about what happened and how they felt about the experience. Often that first response quickly de-escalated the situation and helped bring the student to a calmer place. Once that was achieved, it then allowed me to point out to the disgruntled student, who was now ready to listen, the benefit of using more constructive ways to communicate their grievance, especially if they wanted an opportunity to be heard. In those situations, it's best not to take what students say or do personally but, when needed, remain at a physically safe distance while students are in venting mode.

Teachers are better positioned to help students transition from maladjusted to fully adjusted. So let's never lose faith in any student's capacity to learn. If we let them know what goals to aspire to and explain how to achieve those goals when dealing with academic, social, or behavioral challenges, it will result in improved performance outcomes in all areas.

What All Teachers Have in Common

The influx of new students assigned to every teacher at the start of a new school year always requires them to push a "reset" on the first day of school. Every student they welcome at the start of a new year is different from the population of students they taught the previous school year. Despite having the advantage of amassing years of experience developing class routines and cultural norms, even mid-level and veteran teachers are faced with many "unknowns" upon the arrival of new and different personalities.

Most assuredly, some students will test the veracity of their teacher's management skills, which took years to refine. In some cases, students who arrive with complex issues may experience difficulty adapting to expectations during the initial transition phase. As tempting as it may be to blame the students, it is not the responsibility of students to instinctively know what is expected of them or how to respond to those expectations. However, routines and clearly stated expectations embedded in classroom management practices are learnable and necessary. Most students are capable of quickly adapting to routines and expectations. Knowing what those routines and expectations are provides a source of predictability and comfort. They also want assurances that the adult in the room is in charge, while also being accessible, respectful, and friendly to all students. Rapport between students and teachers truly matters.

Setting Expectations Is Key to Well-Managed Classrooms

If you have recently visited classrooms where students were actively engaged in learning, in that moment you were fortunate to witness one of the most effective techniques for managing an entire classroom. Lessons designed to engage all students in learning are one of the essential keys to maintaining a well-run class environment. Other evidence of quality instruction will be students' being unfazed by the presence of visitors; meaning they may quickly glance at guests, but then return to the task at hand. Students who are not easily distracted or do not require redirecting back onto task are tuned in to learning. Odds are those classes will also show that little if any instructional time is devoted to addressing disruptive behaviors.

Ask many of those same teachers how their school year began, and you may be surprised to learn how many of them encountered challenges with getting every student on board with conforming to expectations. As difficult as it may be to imagine while visiting classrooms that appear to be, and really are, run well—which is visibly evident in students' familiarity with routines that have seamless and fluid transitions from one subject to the next—it's all been supported by unstated yet explicitly understood expectations. In the early days, seasoned teachers expect that a considerable amount of time and attention will have to be devoted to socially orienting all students to their new class and teacher. Even well-managed classrooms led by teachers who focus on instructional practices may encounter new students who may require more time to learn and gradually become acclimated to behavioral expectations. Most notable are students who arrive either developmentally unprepared, due to the absence of social guidance, or lacking exposure to socially acceptable interactions with peers. Some may have developed the habit of responding defiantly to people in positions of authority.

But let's pause for a moment, and resist the temptation to label a student "maladjusted" if they are among those behaving defiantly. In fairness to children of any age, it is the behavior, and not they, that is maladjusted. And since behaviors, under the right set of circumstances, can significantly improve, we owe it to them to refrain from labeling them. Labeling has a tendency of sticking over prolonged periods and in some cases eventually taking on permanence—even if, over time, a student's behavior no longer mirrors the initial conduct that earned him or her the label. As a teacher and school leader, I know this to be true, based on having successfully worked with many students who initially presented with some of the most challenging behaviors, some of which bordered on reprehensible. But over time, with the help of repeated reminders about expectations—coupled with acknowledgment of their positive efforts and, when needed, behavioral performance reports identifying specific expectations—many students gradually embraced school policies. Their successful transformation was attributed to their being surrounded by consistent expectations uniformly communicated in a respectful manner. For most students, positive recognition of appropriate behaviors usually resulted in an increase in good behaviors.

Students Are Environmentalists

The existence of classroom policies posted and discussed are rendered moot if they are enforced unfairly, haphazardly, or not at all. Often the strongest indicator of how seriously policies and expectations are taken by students is their behavioral response, which generally reveals the degree of effectiveness teachers have with enforcing them. Students' behaviors are usually a fairly good barometer of the existence, or absence, of the behavioral parameters in the classroom. If students detect little effort is applied in holding all students accountable at all times, the credibility of boundaries will be tested. The testing of boundaries, if not responded to right away and in ways that make clear what behaviors are acceptable and unacceptable, forms students' perceptions about what they can or cannot get away with, and this becomes their first assessment of the classroom environment. For teachers who spend a great deal of time, early and often at the start of the school year, exerting time and energy establishing and reinforcing expectations, the benefits usually evolve in the way students respond, particularly if reinforcement of expectations is done in a judicious manner that is fair and equitable. Establishing respectful and socially appropriate classroom norms helps cultivate predictability, which strengthens and sustains routines.

Credibility of classroom policies is determined by a teacher's willingness to work diligently with students to help them understand and achieve expectations related to those policies. Enforcement also has to be done equitably. Students' perception of fairness is shaped by how often teachers select the "carrot over the stick" (please don't take that literally) and who among them most frequently receives one or the other. Equitable enforcement of policies means using a balanced system of positive recognition afforded to all students when their behavior warrants acknowledging and holding them accountable. But rule infractions have to be responded to in accordance with the same process of accountability for all students. While it may be tempting to forgive occasional and uncharacteristic outbursts from students who generally conduct themselves in compliance with classroom policies, in the early days and weeks of a new school year every initial incident from any student has to be perceived as warranting compassionate intervention to help them navigate their way through whatever is upsetting them. To not see some students as worthy of compassionate intervention the first time their behavior is disruptive while others are seen as worthy will be the first sign of division that could potentially create an unintended chasm among students.

Avoiding appearance of preferring one or some students over others can be achieved by maintaining professionalism and, as much as possible, consistently, fairly, and respectfully interacting with students in humane and compassionate ways that allow them to retain their dignity. Developmentally, where some students in crisis may also be at a fragile stage in their emotional growth cycle, what makes those moments most memorable is the indelible impression they were left with as a result of how their teacher handled the situation.

The real test of the stability of any class environment is what happens when a teacher has to step away from the classroom for some reason. At the start of the school year, it's advisable to create a buddy system with a neighboring teacher. On those occasions when you must leave the room, you can ask another teacher to keep an ear open during the period, which should be kept very short, while you're away. Informing the class about your brief departure and your intention of leaving the door open to allow the teacher next door to supervise from a distance can be helpful. Upon your return, be sure to check in with your neighbor to inquire how your students performed during your absence. If it's good news, praise and thank the students for being capable of independently maintaining good behavior. And because success often begets more success, showing them how proud you are for what they accomplished in your absence will likely motivate them to uphold their reputation whenever you leave the room. But remember to convey your appreciation. Students appreciate being appreciated.

Why Students Owe Teachers No Favors

If you request something as a personal favor to you, you're creating a culture of relying on their allegiance to you instead of classroom standards. This leads to confusion and an environment of unpredictability. Successful teachers gain the respect of students by ensuring that students are beholden to performance expectations and clear boundaries articulated in the policies. In those classrooms, students are surrounded by highly structured routines, and the teacher constantly works with students to help facilitate behavioral habits that foster a healthy and respectful coexistence. The real test is to see whether students maintain conduct contributing to healthy and respectful coexistence when they are not under the direct supervision of adults.

Students Dispensing M&M's

Investing in student learning and motivating students to perceive themselves as achievers, academically and behaviorally, also is influenced by well-managed classroom settings. While not often spoken of, what undergirds the foundation of continued success is the dispensing of generous amounts of positive feedback—but not with candy or other enjoyable edible treats. The M&M's I'm referring to are the kind where teachers who are willing to express appreciation to their students, in return receive the gratification of getting Many & More of that kind of performance from them.

What if What You Said Didn't Matter Because of How It Was Said

Teacher preparation, organization, and communication style (with students, parents, and colleagues) matter. All influence performance outcomes. Policies, rules, and enforcement of expectations may be present in classrooms, but cultivating exceptional classrooms can be greatly undermined by a teacher's style of communication.

A well-managed classroom is an environment where the teacher is an effective communicator, facilitator of instruction, mediator, and role model. Teachers set a tone with their demeanor and style of communication. When they explain the class parameters and make clear the *do's* and *don'ts* and class policies, students are listening to words being said. They are particularly attuned to the way those words are spoken. Some teachers and other school staff tend to take liberties by being playful in ways that are perceived as sarcastic, or they encroach up to and beyond the lines of revealing a student's personal business. Infringement can take many forms, but it is out of bounds for any staff member to violate a student's sense of personal boundaries by assuming it's okay to joke, out loud and in the presence of anyone else, but especially the students' classmates, about something personal to them. Too many adults in positions of authority think their position entitles them to say whatever they want, however they wish, and to whomever is present. Even those with the best of intentions and when speaking in a playful manner do not realize how they are negatively influencing student perceptions about them.

Indicators of how well students are buying into the classroom culture of respect are reflected in interactions between students. Students often imitate, mock, or repeat what they see and hear. When conversations between teachers and students are relived in other classrooms, or when students go home and share how their day went with adult family members, the responses may be appalled looks and comments such as, "Wait. Your teacher said what?" Not surprisingly, these are followed with a call to the school principal the next day. When the principal then reaches out to have a "word with you" about the comments students heard and then shared with others, choose that moment to listen carefully and without being defensive. Then immediately alter your behavior. Typically, from that moment on, depending upon how egregious your comments either were or were perceived to be, you will be under much scrutiny. Communication style encompasses everything a teacher and other adults say and do. Of course, when asked, you will want an opportunity to share the intentions of your words and remarks, but the damage has been already been done because, regardless of how you intended what you said to be heard, the person on the receiving end perceived it differently. Apologies to the student who felt offended may be warranted. Students generally appreciate knowing we sometimes make mistakes too. How we decide to address our mistakes often matters even more than the remarks that caused someone to feel bad or uncomfortable. Apologies provide an opportunity to push the *reset* button, enabling both parties to recover. So often apologies can help accelerate the healing process.

Detecting Fissures

The absence of expectations, or the manner in which expectations are communicated, can unravel classrooms quickly. Teachers have to be facilitators of learning. However, we frequently assume references to "learning" mean only academic instruction. If teachers do not develop the skills necessary to facilitate student learning of socially appropriate behaviors, it usually leaves classrooms teetering toward instability. Establishing credibility by being a trusted leader of a classroom cultivates comfort among populations of students during the early days of getting acclimated to one another. The process of orienting students to routines in the first days of a new school year integrates style of communication with the process of explaining policies, routines, and expectations. When information is delivered in ways that are unclear, opaque, meek, or apologetic, some students may interpret the communication style differently; but collectively, the majority of students may conclude it lacks the convincing authoritative tone they have become accustomed to expecting.

You may recall an earlier mention that students are intuitive about their classroom environment, capable of assessing the veracity of policies and then distinguishing between real and imagined guardrails related to those policies. Based on the level of veracity, students then behave in accordance with the level of credible enforcement of those guardrails. In fact, most students' behaviors are in response to how effectively or poorly their teacher manages their class. Several students are also innately endowed with an ability to detect performance fissures. Performance fissures are usually easy to detect in weakly delivered threats, repeated directives that, when ignored, cause rapid elevation of decibels in a teacher's voice. If students are amused with getting a rise out of teachers unable to maintain some modicum of professional composure during challenging moments, at times they will then purposely escalate their inappropriate behavior to nudge the teacher's behavior closer to the abyss of hysteria. Their success will be evident in verbal commands spewed in screeches accompanied by facial and physical behaviors that clearly indicate their teacher is indeed on the precipice of *losing it*. Some students feel sympathy or empathy watching their teacher coming undone. Others are terrified by the spectacle because teachers are not supposed to have meltdowns, let alone in the presence of students. Then there will always be one or more opportunists intrigued by how easy it is to trigger the process of peeling away the façade of a teacher appearing to be in control. In fact, fascination in the ability to manipulate most adults falsely masquerading as being in charge can fuel the temptation of students to widen fissures and openly expose the true status of feckless leadership. Teachers who lack effective communication skills are often unable to facilitate their way through chaotic moments.

Once adults' fragile fissures are exposed, it's natural for students to conclude that some adults in positions of leadership are marginally pretending to be in a position of authority. Under those circumstances, teachers, especially new ones, need—but should never have to ask—to be rescued. We may want the luxury of thinking that, after teachers decide to leave teaching, the wounds experienced in teaching will dissipate and these former teachers will gradually recover to someone resembling who they were before they entered the teaching profession. Unfortunately, that is untrue for too many. Those who experience such a disastrous tenure should receive counseling immediately upon their departure; and the district that failed to intervene and prevent their professional collapse should be fully responsible for all counseling session fees incurred. It is the district's responsibility to make them a whole person again, to restore their health after they experienced either tragic outcomes due to excessive poor treatment, or else some manner of harm that could have been avoided if they had been given help when it was requested. And it's another reason for the professional services of classroom management specialists.

The Contagiousness of Generosity

Generally, when students are asked how their day in school went, the response might be a shrug of their shoulders or else utterances indicating it was okay. The true assessment of how some portion of their day transpired may come at unexpected moments, like dinner, when they blurt out loud something about a compliment they received from a particular teacher. Being subtle about positive interactions between themselves and teachers they may admire is an important revelation. Teacher-student rapport matters in education. Teachers who openly express appreciation to students who conduct themselves in a respectful manner with their fellow students or during interactions with any adult, know the value of praising students.

The habit of praising students seems to come naturally to some teachers and other staff members. Unfortunately, the act of publicly praising or openly showing appreciation to students and colleagues in schools does not get the kind of attention it deserves because teachers are rarely shown expressions of appreciation. Teaching programs at colleges and universities should include topics related to building rapport with students and colleagues. The act of sprinkling generous doses of kindness by way of compliments and expressions of "Nice job!" are more impactful than most people realize. They tend to make people want to continue to bask in spotlights. Students are no exception. They just may want it done in subtle forms, especially when among their peers. After all, they have reputations to protect.

What can be even more gratifying is when students begin to mimic kind interactions they have experienced or witnessed. Whether or not students appear to be doing it in jest, mimicking or mocking kindness may be evidence that your behaviors are worthy of remembering. Remember the advice passed along through many generations that "imitation is the sincerest form of flattery"? It can also be transformational. Find ways to welcome and embrace those moments. But have your sensitivity antenna raised so you can distinguish between harmless and playful mocking or the form of mocking that is unintentionally mistaken as publicly embarrassing or humiliating.

Conversely, don't hesitate to respectfully push back at those who attempt to humiliate you. But do so calmly and respectfully, whether privately or in the presence of others. If any act attempting to embarrass a teacher or student is done in public spaces, so too should efforts to respectfully push back occur in the presence those who witnessed the disrespectful behavior. The objective is not to show or elevate your authority as a teacher or staff member. It's to show students that you too are a human being entitled to being respected at all times. As a human being, wearing a title of "teacher" does not exempt anyone from needing to show you respect. Use the incident as a teachable moment to allow everyone to walk away without having to lose their dignity.

Getting caught acting decisively but without coating the situation in condescension or anger will cause some chatter throughout the school. If the incident is perceived and accurately reported as it actually occurred, your reputation could be greatly enhanced. Among students and staff members who witness the exchange are people who will likely appreciate and admire the way you chose to handle the situation. It also serves as a model. It is rare for students to encounter respectful responses to remarks that were made in disrespectful ways. Acts of respect under any circumstance are a sign of generosity. But conveying respect in response to being disrespected is an example of how generosity can come in many different forms. In my previous book, *America's Educational Crossroads*, the topic of schools being incubators for bullying was discussed. Schools can also be incubators for acts of generosity. It can happen when adults model generosity.

Over time, the process of extending kindness toward others can become a habit that eventually evolves into a normalized expectation of every person. But generous deeds and words appeal to students because they beget a desire for students to earn more recognition. After all, many students do live to please the teachers they admire. Sometimes that admiration appears in the form of playfully mocking their teacher. In those moments, students may simply be paying homage to the attributes they see, like, and trust in someone with whom they desire to build a rapport. Look for evident signs of generosity among students. If their social interactions with their peers include empathy, compassion, encouragement, advising peers to steer away from trouble, or a willingness to intervene on behalf of others targeted by would-be bullies, it's an indication of how generous acts of kindness are embedded in your school's culture.

Why New Teachers Never Need to Apologize

The successful launch of each school year involves hours of classroom management planning. Do you know of any first-year teacher who arrives on their first day with a foolproof classroom management blueprint? The idea that each knows where to start and understands the broad range of responsibilities that await them is ludicrous and unfair. It helps to have a list indicating tasks to be done, and in what order. Arranging class furniture, taking an inventory of education materials, and attending to the room's décor are usually the easy part of the early days. Planning lessons is one of the most challenging areas for first-year teachers because they are inadequately informed about the correlation between engagement in lessons and disruptive behaviors. When some students feel disconnected from lessons, it can set off any number of emotions. Falling behind is a very frustrating experience. Sadly, many new teachers are not even aware of signs exhibited by students who are left behind, or how to address them. This is a very common problem. Managing a classroom requires a multilevel classroom-management plan that promotes and builds student self-esteem. Few new teachers are aware of how integral a student's sense of belonging is to their ability to comprehend what is being taught.

The challenge of establishing classroom norms is made more confounding because most new teachers initially do not understand the magnitude of the multilevel planning and the scale of work needed to prepare their classrooms and lessons before students arrive. Access to a full-time classroom management specialist to train teachers how to develop, while gaining familiarity with, each of the components of a multilevel classroom-management plan would allow them to proceed with more confidence. One cannot stress enough the importance of training new teachers how to assess different levels of severity of incidents and having an awareness of what would be the most appropriate intervention technique to use. Retaining new teachers requires training them to be prepared for many possibilities. When new teachers are prepared, their levels of anxiety can be significantly reduced. A less-anxious teacher can serve to reassure a sense of safety among all students.

The Connection Between a Student's Self-Esteem and Class Culture

One common mistake made during efforts to create the ideal classroom culture is to think the process begins and ends with setting up the physical structure of classrooms, sharing policies and expectations, distributing class schedules, and coordinating icebreaker activities to socially acquaint students with one another. Those steps are necessary during the initial stages of setting up classrooms. But it is the dynamics of social interactions during lessons and unstructured time that greatly influence class culture. Since students spend most of each school day engaged in lessons, how they experience learning forms their perspective about the culture of their class.

What anchors and stabilizes a class's culture is what occurs during learning time. Well-prepared lessons that do not fully engage all students can derail the stability of any class. A few other potential obstacles are related to a teacher's chosen method of instruction and delivery. Now let's add another layer impacting class cultures. The presence of students who possess different levels of social tolerance towards their peers will impact the quality of social interactions during and beyond lessons. Then there is the broad range of students' interest in learning, spanning from highly uninterested in learning to enthusiastic and eager to engage in learning. Successfully engaging all students, represented across a broad spectrum of the educationally willing, in lessons is one of the most challenging and important priorities in all classrooms.

One key to investing all students in learning is the teacher's enthusiasm for teaching. When students observe a teacher's authentic passion for teaching, it can have a contagious effect. Class cultures need the presence of magnetic personalities. Stylistically, teachers communicate differently from one another. While some have a more laid-back presence but occasionally surprise students by showing their playful nature, others have a different kind of magnetism. Whatever style you arrive to school with, let the students appreciate your intention of establishing your presence. Concede your leadership role to no one. Why? Because showing up with a demeanor making it evident you intend to show your passion for teaching and conveying appreciation for the opportunity to bring your students along for the ride will make the day even more special. The element of surprise is an advantage teachers have. Students' perception of teachers influences their level of enthusiasm for attending school.

If much of the attention is paid to one central figure in the class, it takes the pressure from students who are socially shy, while engaging the attention of socially outgoing students. At the start of every school year, establishing cultural norms that foster respectful coexistence among students requires teachers to be the central figure, capable of drawing every student's attention. Over time, teachers can assess the social temperature of the class and decide when it's time for them to dial back their alpha or alphette presence. As students show signs of settling in with class routines and demonstrate they are capable of living within the boundaries of socially acceptable expectations, teachers can relinquish some of the need to be the central figure. But remain ready to reassert the stronger presence role when needed. Teachers are the most essential anchors in any class. Teachers who are uncomfortable with owning the leadership role and unprepared to assert themselves are likely to spend more time addressing behavioral issues.

Conveying a strong presence and enthusiasm for teaching will give new teachers an advantage, but that alone will not maintain the stability of classrooms. New and veteran teachers must recognize the different ways students in their classes experience learning. Teacher personalities matter more if they learn to attend to the educational needs of students who experience challenges with learning.

If it were possible to diagram the x and y coordinates to track the rate of frequency at which instructional frustration intersects with behavioral issues, it might help us to better see the early signs of students disconnecting from lessons. Instructional frustration is generally an indication of students experiencing difficulty in understanding what is being taught. Some early signs of instructional frustration, which precedes and then triggers learning frustration, can be manifested in student detachment from lessons. Signs of detachment may be anger, embarrassment, or the decision to just totally shut down. Unfortunately, during periods of detachment, most students do not feel safe to raise their hand in the presence of their peers and say out loud, "I need help" or "I don't get it." In some cases, even after a student summons the courage to openly acknowledge they need help, new teachers are likely to repeat the information the same way originally stated.

Unable to process the information after the teacher's second explanation, which simply repeated the same words used in the first explanation, is an awkward moment experienced by students. If the teacher detects a look of confusion or reads the student's body language indicating they still did not understand, the teacher assumes repeating the same information more slowly or in smaller portions would probably be more helpful. Little is spoken about how students learn social survival skills to appease their teachers. Preferring to avoid discomfort for teachers who repeat information that is as useless as the first time it was shared, students politely retreat so as not to prolong the awkward situation. The process of extracting themselves is how they remove the spotlight away from them and the teacher. Insisting the teacher find another way to explain what the student had made clear they do not understand is not an option. Students who politely nod their head to signal affirmation that they get it, is how they acquiesce. That approach is common in many classrooms. It's an exit strategy students use to help them and their teacher save face. It's also a moment of deciding to forfeit their education. Other students observing the exchange conclude that any student's request for help is a fruitless endeavor. Eventually, students learn not to raise their hand for clarification. Teachers unskilled in diverse methods of instruction resort to the only response they currently know. What the teacher probably never notices is the number of eye-rolls shared among students as soon as his/her back is turned when returning to the chalkboard.

In recalling my first year as a teacher possessing a small arsenal of strategies in my limited instructional tool kit, it helped me recognize the plight of new teachers caught in the same scenario. I too lacked diverse methods needed to make instruction accessible to all students. When, as a new special education teacher standing at the board and seeing several students raise their hand and say, almost in unison, "I don't get it," I felt incredulous that they were unable to understand what I was saying. I was that teacher who repeated the information in the same way it was shared the first time, because I just could not fathom why they were not able to grasp my careful way of showing and telling them. Students just looked away without uttering another word.

I took that as a sign they finally understood. I was relieved, until they turned in their assignments and I saw evidence to the contrary. They had not understood. Like so many of my first-year colleagues in those moments, I was flustered. But with no immediate solution available to dig myself out of a hole, frustration began to emerge. My frustration was recognizing how unprepared I was to be standing in front of students who relied on me to teach them. What a time to discover my instructional deficiencies! Motivated to be a better teacher for the sake of my students, and to recover as quickly as possible from a terribly embarrassing situation, I immediately sought the support of veteran colleagues, who generously gave of their time. They also shared instructional tools they had acquired during their many years of teaching.

What I experienced during my first few years as a teacher is at the nexus of why I chose to advocate for professional development support for teachers, but especially new teachers. Discovering how my level of instructional deficiencies intertwined with the learning frustrations experienced by my students influenced my commitment to gain proficiency. I am not exaggerating when I describe how much I truly benefited from gaining instructional proficiency. The greater my level of proficiency, the better students performed academically. Bolstering student confidence in their ability to learn was another benefit of my efforts to acquire instructional proficiency. It also contributed to a culture of learning unencumbered by fear of making errors. But the turning point for me, as an evolving educator, was learning how to create multiple points of entry to accommodate the diverse range of learning profiles among my students. One useful way to motivate them to participate was to provide lessons designed to attract student interest.

The Challenge of Reframing How Students Perceive and Respond to Errors

Teachers can remove the sting of making errors by preparing students to expect that they will sometimes encounter challenges that will result in making mistakes. Classrooms can cultivate learning practices that elevate taking risks without equating incorrect outcomes with failure. The freedom of escaping the mentality where incorrect answers are absolutely unacceptable requires removing all of the negative connotations students have been taught to perceive as unwelcomed mistakes. If we start by introducing learning as a process that greatly benefits from risk-taking through trial and error, students can start to appreciate that challenges are to be expected and students need not fear what they do not yet know.

Teachers can develop learning safety nets in classes to help students not be afraid of making mistakes. As facilitators, teachers can focus on strategies students can learn to extract themselves from challenging situations, and this will build students' self-esteem. More importantly, teachers should help students become accustomed to encountering challenges. Equipping students with skills to independently navigate their way through solving varying levels of difficult or complex problems strengthens their higher-order-of-thinking skills. The following are some steps that can be taken:

1. Impress upon students the benefits of staying calm and not panicking when they make mistakes.

2. Explain the rules of engagement between teachers and students when the teacher takes on the role of facilitator of learning.
3. Clarify that facilitators are not givers of answers; instead, they facilitate learning through a process that relies on helping students think analytically.
4. Consider creating and sharing a helpful step-by-step instructional manual for independent problem-solving. The instructional manuals should be tailored to the unique elements for each subject and guide students through a process of brainstorming sessions and thinking exercises to develop every student's intellectual ability.
5. Modify, as needed, independent problem-solving steps tailored to students with special needs. Ensuring all students accessibility to independent learning activities, based on level of assistance needed to successfully participate, is how teachers make all students participants in the learning process.
6. Emphasize that learning analytical strategies for examining and extrapolating key information has to become habit forming.
7. Probe students about reasons for their decisions; this is essential for students to gain comfort with justifying their decisions. Having students articulate what influenced their decision, how they came to their conclusion, and why they made the choices they made can lead to an "Aha" moment that reveals where they made a mistake. The ability to find and then self-correct errors is beneficial to the learning process.
8. Redirect students to a track that can net favorable results, when they occasionally veer off course. Probing can be in the form of cues or questions that can serve as helpful hints intended to steer students in the right direction. Students will need to "put on their thinking cap" to interpret the purpose of questions being asked. Students can learn how to probe teachers for more information when needed.
9. Discuss with students, prior to assigning independent work, strategic self-help steps that enable students to independently work their way through complicated problems.
10. Teach students how to rely on their capacity to independently explore and analytically think through challenging moments when they are stuck. Learning how to get unstuck is an integral part of the learning process. The goal is for students to develop intellectual curiosity and self-reliance.
11. Encourage learning through exploration that leads to self-discovery, to enable students to take a more active role in learning.

Students who learn how to take more responsibility for learning will strengthen their self-esteem. Getting used to expecting mistakes while using a learning process that requires learning through trial and error helps students become less dependent on a need to produce the right answer on the first try. Learning safety nets is a form of assurance that students will be granted numerous chances to work-through and solve problems without fear of earning a failing grade. Cultivating exceptional classrooms requires schools and teachers to help students adapt to more rigorous and intellectually challenging learning cultures without fear.

Taking risks, learning through trial and error, is a departure from current pedagogical practices where teachers, textbooks and other educational resources relay information and students regurgitate what they are told. That is not learning. It is developing memorization skills. And it is why many prefer assessments that use *open-ended questions*. Open-ended questions are designed to elicit more detailed responses to questions. Students use their own words instead of providing "yes" or "no" answers. Open-ended questions may be more useful for revealing level of knowledge about topics taught, but it does present difficulty for students experiencing challenges with essay-writing skills. The need to strengthen writing skills should not preclude students from responding to open-ended questions. Assistive technology devices are available for recording student's responses. Having a variety of resources in classrooms to facilitate engagement in learning is how we bring accessibility and equity into the learning process for all students. When students succeed in learning, they are less preoccupied with what grades they receive. Shifting the focus on how we educate students based on their learning profile makes the process of learning memorable and meaningful.

Chasing correct answers for the sake of earning passing grades has taught our students to fear making mistakes. If we set aside the current practice of grading students and instead use some form of standards-based rubric models that specify skills, as well the degree of strength or level of understanding students demonstrate in their acquisition of skills, it finally places emphasis on the real purpose of educating students. It will be a developmental, skill-based learning model. Students need reassurance that the conditions in classrooms are safe spaces that grant them the freedom to give answers that accurately reflect what they know or do not know. In other words, they need to be able to honestly reply to questions. Instead of fearing being right or wrong, students ought to have an education system that utilizes instructional models that give them the leeway to show areas of strength and areas in need of improving. Intellectual capabilities are more likely to flourish in educational conditions that recognize the need to accommodate the various learning styles among students present in classrooms. Learning has to stimulate intellectual thinking and cognitive growth. That should supersede the current educational model where students learn how to memorize and then recite what they are told.

Rescuing Students Who Have Encountered Learning Challenges

If a teacher's first impulse is to step in and give the correct answer whenever students encounter challenges, students are being denied the opportunity to learn. Sometimes learning is a struggle. If students do not acquire thinking habits, which can be learned through the facilitated guidance of teachers, they are generally inclined to not even make a sincere effort. Instead, they acquire the habit of being rescued by their teacher and fall victim of learned helplessness.

Learned helplessness is the result of an act of misguided generosity from teachers or adults who habitually give in. Fearing threats of a potential outburst or disruption, some teachers, at the first sign of a student appearing to be on the verge of expressing frustration or threatening to no longer participate in lessons, immediately use a reliable default response that will settle the student down; they provide the correct answer. Instead of learning content, students learn how to manipulate teachers. Students who succeed in shifting the paradigm of control away from teachers usually have discovered the parameters of their teacher's comfort zone. Classroom management that occasionally reveals lapses in teachers' remaining in control is often most prevalent during instruction. Evidence that students are in control can be seen in the high rate of student dependency upon teachers to intervene and allow students who are struggling to discontinue participating in lessons or doing assignments.

Interventions intended to de-escalate impending meltdowns by excusing students from learning are evidence that a teacher is willing to lower expectations, and that circumvents a student's ability to meet educational standards. Learning content is just one level of education. Learning how to embrace challenges requires students to be able to recover from mistakes and teachers to refrain from the temptation to provide students with answers. Teachers can provide road maps to help students think their way through steps that will reveal how the error occurred, apply the remedy needed, and then proceed forward. Withholding answers in exchange for learning self-instructional processes is how to keep students from falling victim to learned helplessness. Essentially, learning is as much about students possessing strategies that elevate their self-confidence in their ability to independently extract themselves from challenging situations when they feel stuck. Learned helplessness may result in instant gratification of being rescued; but over time, performance outcomes on assessments or tests reveal the truth about what the student has not learned. Receiving repeated feedback in the form of low or failing grades erodes a student's enthusiasm about attending classes and cultivates fragility and lack of confidence. Teachers have to teach students how to encounter and then overcome challenges. Students need opportunities to see themselves as capable of overcoming any and all challenges. That cannot happen if they are constantly being spoon-fed answers. Teachers can reframe student expectations of being rescued by developing ways to help students remain engaged in learning. Breaking the cycle of learned helplessness is the responsibility of teachers. Students can learn to embrace moments of being challenged by enduring challenges without relying on behaviors signaling frustration. Interventions intended to help people addicted to harmful habits, is similar to teachers' needing to break the cycle of co-dependency. In this instance, the harm is preventing students the opportunity to receive an education. We have to help teachers develop healthy classroom cultures that welcome achievements, but we also have to teach students to embrace fearlessness of making errors. It is inside of those spaces that all students generally do well because they don't fear their educational experience. Learning is not synonymous with fear of failure.

Another indication of a healthy classroom culture is when a student complains of earning a lower grade than expected and requests an opportunity have additional time to study and retake the test. The student is speaking from a place of possessing educational aspirations, where they desire to do better and sincerely believe they can. It is their self-esteem that is motivating the request. They believe they can do better, and they just want a chance to prove to themselves that they can. This is a great example of what we should want: more students thinking highly of themselves and what they believe themselves capable of achieving.

Extending Courtesy Beyond Their First Day

For newcomers to the school, early impressions are influenced by how they are made to feel welcome and accepted in their new environment. At the start of every new school year, all students arriving to new classes are, of course, newcomers. Newcomers entering a new grade level require continual attention to their social and emotional well-being. However, that is not solely the responsibility of the teacher. All students have a role in contributing to the well-being of one another. Well-orchestrated and practiced routines need to be established at the start of every school year. Teachers also need to provide guardrails to make clear what the safe parameters are to help students navigate their way around the class and one another. However, the social high points of a student's day—which are generally lunch and recess—can become hazard zones that challenge students to independently remain within the guardrails made clear in their classrooms. There is simply no way to constantly monitor conditions that make everyone feel accepted in all common and less supervised spaces. But that cannot deter schools from exploring ways to develop habits of good character that instill in students their need to contribute to maintaining a safe and welcoming environment for themselves and their peers, at all times and in all spaces.

Emphasis on character building is needed to foster healthy habits of communication and respectful coexistence among students. Because few teachers are aware of or intuitively knowledgeable about strategies to promote respect and resolve conflicts, there are significant gaps in their tool kit for addressing those issues. Yet it's commonly known that classroom cohesion requires respectful social interactions. Social interactions are the actual glue that foster and then bind highly productive cultures together while producing a feeling of safety for everyone. Safe cultures are the by-product of welcoming spaces. Welcoming spaces reduce fears of students' exposing their inadequacies. Identifying vulnerable peer pressure points can be greatly assisted with the support of classroom management specialists familiar with the variety of student comfort zones—particularly in the most vulnerable areas, like taking risks among their peers and teachers. Cultivating classroom norms is interdependent upon character development. Students' empathy and compassion for others is one of the most reassuring signs that their classroom is a safe and welcoming space for everyone, when everyone shows a willingness to contribute to ensuring the safety of others.

Teachers are the primary facilitator of assuring everyone's well-being, particularly during lessons when students tend to fear being judged by their peers. At the slightest indication or sign teachers see or hear about students being ridiculed for not knowing something, teachers have to learn how to shield their students' self-esteem. One way is to immediately convey that classrooms are meant to welcome a variety of responses, whether correct or incorrect. Another way is to initially explain to students and then, when needed, repeatedly remind them, that incorrect answers are not only welcome but appreciated because it shows areas in need of additional instruction. Students who make an effort to answer honestly must be valued. That can happen when teachers openly express their appreciation to students willing to help them become better teachers. When students see teachers embracing errors as important revelations for how they can improve the quality of instruction, demonstrating imperfections becomes normalized. Acceptance of imperfections presents opportunities for improvement without judgment for students and their teachers.

Classroom Management Specialist

As a resource and facilitator of students learning socially appropriate skills, teachers may find it useful to prepare an appropriate example of something similar they experienced as a student at the same grade level. When teachers show their human side, they earn points for being willing to share a vulnerable moment from when they were their students' age. The example should be selected wisely, though; A teacher doesn't want to be harnessed with something they wish they hadn't shared; a 10-month school year is a long time to be reminded of an unintended blooper. Find a trusted colleague and test your example on them. You're welcome.

For more about the roles and responsibilities of the classroom management specialist, see page 182 in the appendix.

CHAPTER 10

Inclusion Support Specialist

How to Cultivate Socially Appropriate Habits

TEACHERS ARE RESPONSIBLE FOR CULTIVATING SOCIALLY appropriate habits. Students need modeling examples of what is meant by being respectful. Often the best thing a teacher can do is lead by example. Using interactions with students and colleagues in the presence of students, who watch everything their teachers say and do anyway, is modeling socially appropriate behaviors.

Another equally important process of cultivating socially appropriate behaviors is for teachers to intentionally provide acceptable standards that will engender each student's capacity to show empathy for others. Acts of kindness that come in the form of encouraging instead of discouraging one another are also ways to cultivate healthy interactions. Fundamentally, from the start of each school year, attending to foundational rules of social engagement is needed. But given the mosaic of culturally and ethnically diverse student populations, understanding how customs vary from one ethnic group to another can start with discussions where all students assigned to a teacher's class are invited to share their customs and explain why they are important. Students have to be viewed through multiple lenses in order to appreciate how diverse they are from one another, beyond their personalities and learning profiles.

Schools are places where students are sent to learn. But what they experience in the day-to-day process of learning greatly influences their ability to learn. That is why educating students, who come from diverse backgrounds and experiences, in a classroom requires teachers to recognize the importance of unifying students under a new classroom landscape where their character growth is nurtured within parameters that make it safe to make and recover from mistakes. Their individual dignity is protected throughout the process of holding them accountable to rule infractions in an environment where class standards and norms were designed to respond to the whole needs of every student.

Strengthening Inclusion Practices in General Education Classrooms

Inclusion specialists in this current century are needed to support teachers of special-needs students in general education classrooms. Since classroom teachers are the primary providers of education to all students—including special education students with Individualized Education Plans (IEPs), 504 Education Plans, or ESL (English as a Second Language) Plans—inclusion specialists are needed to facilitate changes of instructional methods used by teachers. (See "What Is ESL" at *ESLDirectory.com* and also "IEP vs. 504 Plans: What's the Difference?" at *Understood.org/articles/en/the-difference-between-ieps-and-504-plans*.) General education teachers assigned special education students need guidance in understanding the particular needs of the variety of disabled populations in their classrooms. Individual Education Plans (IEPs), describing methods of instruction related to each student's learning profile, how to fully integrate students in lessons, use of assistive technology to enhance learning, modifications to lessons where needed, and other forms of support, often lack the level of attention needed, due to lack of familiarity and insufficient resources.

Inclusion specialists are needed to train general education teachers, who are rarely if ever trained to work with populations of students represented across the broad spectrum of disabled individuals. Transferring documents into the hands of general education teachers without extensive and ongoing consultation from special education experts is an unreliable process. However, in many schools this is exactly how the process of informing general education teachers is done. They are left to read and interpret what each component in an IEP makes explicit. Complications arise when general education teachers do not recognize unfamiliar terms. Of even greater concern is when there is no one available to explain what those terms mean and how to put them into practice by successfully integrating the student's social, emotional, and physical needs with lessons planned to promote full participation.

Diversification of learning resources extends to many elements of a well-run classroom. Expectations that are made clear are greatly enhanced when teachers couple the information shared with informing students about how they can achieve those expectations. It's important to remember that goals will not be attained at the same rate or pace by everyone.

Think of the process of achieving something as requiring ladders built with multiple rungs to help students advance, but at their own pace. Some students may be able to advance up the ladder using every other rung, while others may need to use every rung available to achieve forward progress.

Communication, the glue that binds everyone, is an effective resource when delivered and received respectfully. Similar to the metaphor of the rungs on the ladder, communication may need to be modified and dispensed differently and in accordance to each student's current level of what he or she can take, process, and understand. So much hinders on what each student's individual maturational state of mind can handle at this stage of development. Each needs time to learn, adjust, occasionally flounder, and then recover without having sacrificed his or her dignity. Whether interactions are social or during lessons, parameters for expectations are going to be needed.

The ability of students to achieve expectations during instruction depends on lesson planning and method of delivery. If students are assigned work to be done through collaboration with other students, their ability to successfully complete tasks will depend on what forms of communication teachers use to share their expectations and provide instruction. At the start of lessons, teachers generally use verbal communication to explain tasks, the process required to complete assignments, and other essential information. Teachers can follow up their verbal communication with written and clearly stated step-by-step directions, mirroring what has been verbally communicated, as a means of reiterating directions. Providing written directions promotes use of visual guidance for students who would benefit from having access to directions they can repeatedly reference visually. It often helps to condense steps down to the simplest wording onto an index card and tape the card to a student's desk; or students can be sent a text on their electronic devices. Students who struggle with reading can be accommodated by replacing words with pictures. And for those who are impacted by a hearing impairment or whose primary language is not English, technology can be upgraded to accommodate digital translation and interpretation resources. However, there are currently instances where inaccuracies, such as pictures not matching words, exist in the digital terrain, making it apparent that the field of technology needs to continue developing reliable resources aligned with every teacher's ability to support students in need of adaptive resources, so these students can achieve at the highest educational standards.

Newcomers from other countries experience learning impediments, not because they are incapable of learning, but because widely available electronic devices and digital translation tools are either too costly or districts in many communities are unaware of free models, like Translator. Translation apps are becoming more accessible to teachers, students, and family members of newcomers from other non-English-speaking countries, and to students who are deaf or hard of hearing (DHH). Tools designed to translate information enhance a DHH student's ability to learn by "bridging communication gaps, supporting accessible classroom learning with live captioning, cross-language understanding, and multilingual casual conversations to help with student integration" (Using Microsoft Translator for Education, Support.microsoft.com).

How We Include the Broad Spectrum of Student Populations

Public schools are in many ways similar to the United Nations (UN), where people of all nationalities are represented from around the globe. Why it did not occur to us decades ago to invest in translation equipment similar to models used for translation at the UN is quite curious. Our country is one of the most globally diverse populated countries, yet we lag behind in enhancing accessibility to education due to a digital divide that reveals another contributing factor to our educational inequities. The new wave of digital translation programs in education may in the near future net promising results in districts that are partnering with various companies and organizations that envisioned ways to enhance partnerships between schools, students, and families. Imagine how valuable digital translation apps will be when those tools are available for use to students taking state-mandated standardized assessments. The removal of language barriers in our education system will support our pluralistic society that welcomes people from every nation who traveled to this country in search of their own more promising futures.

Planning lessons designed to deliver instruction through multiple modalities—auditory, visual, tactile, and with the aid of translation resources—will be how we successfully include the broad range of learners present in every classroom. Any form of communication that effectively connects students to content and expands their knowledge enhances each student's ability to access information they can cognitively process in ways familiar to them.

The availability of an inclusion specialist for weekly consultation, or daily when needed, will enable a systematic monitoring and assessment of degree of progress achieved by each special education student. This is the process needed to educate and acclimate general education teachers in how to prepare for quality instruction and full inclusion of all students with IEPs. The successful integration of special education students into general education classrooms now designated as inclusion classrooms comes with great risk when personnel knowledgeable about the diverse and in-depth needs of those individuals to support their successful transition and ensure sustainable achievement in all classes are also not included. If general education teachers are assigned disabled and capable learners among their population of general education students, it is unfair to both teachers and special-needs students to assume that these teachers possess the capacity to include special-needs students without their having had special education training.

Here's a not-so-well-known fact: many general education students not identified as needing additional support adapt to learning challenges by relying on ways to compensate for impediments that they too experience. It's just that their peers with special needs may require assistive technology, more physical space in classrooms to navigate their way around, additional and different audio devices to hear better, and modifications to instruction to support their ability to learn. Similar to students who need to wear glasses or use hearing aids, but on a greater and sometimes far more challenging scale, disabled students may need more but often are not adequately equipped with the right resources to successfully participate in a general education setting. Thus, they are unable to navigate around or through obstacles that prevent them from fully participating in general education settings. It is in this way that the general public unknowingly blames disabled people, or holds them responsible for their condition. It is insulting and lacks sensitivity. Our ignorance about how we further victimize people already physically challenged—and often made less visible or valued in our society—is an indication of a need to reset our educational model so we can stop infringing on the educational rights of any citizen. Inclusion support specialists are vital to the success of including students in general education classrooms because they can assess the specific types of resources the students will need and help general education teachers familiarize themselves with those resources. An inclusion specialist can help teachers prepare classes so transitions will be as smooth as possible and will be welcoming for disabled students.

Preparing peers, in advance, for the eventual arrival of a classmate with physical or other disabilities is a very delicate issue. Rarely do we know what can be said and how much is appropriate to reveal. But preparing classmates to welcome another classmate with obvious differences is a priority. Inclusion specialists have to be capable of helping teachers with messaging. Inclusion is challenging for everyone, but the greatest burden falls on those students with obvious features or behaviors that are noticeably different from those of other students. Character development is a maturational process that occurs at different stages for each student. However, school staff members sometimes have to frame narratives that intentionally emphasize good character attributes like compassion. Kids can observe something that may initially seem different, because in fact it is, but then quickly get past that moment because they are resilient and

Inclusion Support Specialist

often quicker to accept differences than adults. But they may need to be intentionally and carefully led in conversations about how they might initially see someone with physical features or behaviors obviously different from theirs. Those conversations should also include ways to learn empathy for others by asking them to consider how they might feel to be constantly stared at, or to understand how being treated with indifference can lead to insecurity and fragility.

The same messaging has to spread throughout the school like a blanket because everyone has to be conditioned to be thoughtful, respectful, and welcoming, but without overdoing it. Overdoing it can come in the form of extreme acts of kindness, which, while intended to convey being nice, creates awkwardness for the student receiving any excessive act meant to be kind. An example of cultivating an exceptional school culture is a school that fully welcomes and makes clear that, while differences exist, they will not interfere with extending efforts to welcome and signal acceptance to everyone who walks or wheels themselves through the entrance doors. Since disabled people have always been deprioritized, many schools are not accessible to members of the disabled community. In many cases, getting through doors will not guarantee their ability to navigate multiple floors, use restrooms, or participate in communal meals. Those attributes previously referenced deserve a chance to be seen and appreciated. Inclusion support specialists have to be capable of leading initiatives that unite all students and staff to advance the school's culture of acceptance and respect for everyone.

Acceptance of diverse differences in the way we look or behave will undoubtedly cause curiosity about something or a feature seen for the first time. Instinctively, we need to look to satisfy our curiosity. That is normal and human. But it's also okay to advise students to try not to stare too long. Under certain circumstances, we may look and notice something and then instinctively our reflex tells us to quickly look away. While not the same but applicable in some way, when some people accidentally grab and put on different socks that don't match, people give them a break by noticing and then politely looking away or deciding to say nothing to avoid embarrassing those of us who do occasionally wear mismatched socks. Although some of us may do so on purpose. It's really no big thing. And it's likely how every person attending their school would like to be received.

For more about the roles and responsibilities of the inclusion support specialist, see page 187 in the appendix.

CHAPTER 11

Academic Achievement Specialist

Schools Need Academic Achievement Specialists

THE MOST PROMISING OPPORTUNITY TO TRACK AND OVERCOME learning gaps is for schools to designate an academic achievement specialist. An academic achievement specialist, who oversees and monitors student academic performances throughout the school, is needed to support teachers and other staff members in developing a system of collecting and analyzing student work samples to detect learning gaps. Building routines for collecting and assessing a variety of student performance artifacts across all academic and non-academic classes is the initial step needed to identify and remediate learning gaps.

Why Achieving Mastery Should Be the Benchmark for All Students

Academic achievement specialists are key to unifying school staff in support of every school's most important mission: educating students based on the belief that they are all capable of achieving at the highest standards. Initial student performance outcomes that reveal learning and/or instructional deficiencies are not accurate or fair indicators of each student's true level of learning capability. Having adopted the practice of assigning a final grade, then moving on to the next unit without acknowledging what the student's incorrect responses revealed, is the real travesty of our education system. Rather than our appreciating their effort and willingness to share not only what they understood and did not understand, but also what they needed additional time and instruction for in order to achieve mastery, those who earned failing grades were penalized. So were students who earned passing grades, but not A's. Shouldn't the real purpose of education be to provide every student additional instruction until they achieve mastery?

One of the many benefits of an academic achievement specialist is that they can mobilize an entire staff to work collaboratively in instituting remedial instructional plans to address deficiencies. Full-time monitoring of student performance outcomes across all classes is led by the academic achievement specialist, but it is also the responsibility of content, instruction, inclusion, classroom management, and technology specialists, as well as teachers and ancillary staff members (special-needs staff, teaching assistants, and tutors). Monitoring student education performance outcomes has to be viewed through a holistic lens. Ensuring optimal experiences throughout every school year depends on each student's healthy social development growth. Given the interconnection of a student's overall well-being with their academic performance, we should never use academic performance outcomes as the only way to gauge how well students are doing. How often have we dismissed students earning all A's, thinking students "gifted" with brilliance couldn't possibly be harboring insecurities or enduring emotional turmoil like their peers struggling to navigate through complicated and complex circumstances? Why don't geniuses have a right to be fully human?

What Will Be Seen When We Widen the Educational Lens

For staff members to work collaboratively to address the holistic needs of students, every adult must be acclimated and assigned a supportive role with each student to invest in the student's overall educational well-being. Recognizing that student performance outcomes belong to teachers and others who provide services to students enables team participation in a unified remediation plan. This plan prevents the risk of students falling behind academically as well as in tutorial sessions or classes in art and music, where classroom management issues may arise. Even students performing well academically but showing signs of social and emotional difficulty in non-academic areas need a unified remediation plan to extend the use of successful management techniques by every staff member with whom students connect during their school day. Very little has been made of the correlation of what students experience in art, gym, and music classes, where they are generally referred to as "specials," and what they experience the rest of their school day. But it matters.

The Need to Broaden Our Awareness

Social and emotional development is related to a student's self-esteem, which is impacted by the degree of scrutiny they are subjected to by their peers regarding their other skills in gym, art, or music classes. Students judged as having no athletic skills don't just desire to avoid gym class. When peers assess the athletic ability of others in gym classes, it can be a deflating experience for those whose skills don't "measure up" to some arbitrary performance standard. If those who don't "measure up" are branded and ranked among the lowest status of performers, their instinct to want to run for cover or become invisible does not remain in the locker room; it follows them everywhere they go. In some cases, their experiencing of deflation of their self-esteem in gym does carry over into classrooms where they may have at one time enjoyed performance levels worthy of honor roll status; but failing to measure up to standards in the most socially visible arenas brings about feelings of shame and humiliation. The transformation from highly visible, eager, and enthusiastic academic performers, who welcomed opportunities to participate in academic classes, to low-key reticent students who are now too shy to raise a hand and proudly answer questions, is a real issue in schools. High self-esteem is linked with confidence. A student's confidence is influenced by the amount of care they receive through meaningful interactions with compassionate adults who surround them and watch out for their social and emotional well-being. Academic achievement specialists cannot restrict their findings to outcomes of academic performance. All classes shape a student's experience and degree of success throughout each school day.

Bringing to Fruition the Goal of Achieving Proficiency

The need to examine student achievement through an academic lens is to be expected and is why, inside of every school, principals and assistant principals will be ready to welcome academic achievement specialists while holding spreadsheets containing astronomical amounts of data. Among the volume of data are the results of the quarterly, bi-annually, or annually federally mandated standardized tests. The ESSA (Every Student Succeeds Act, preceded by NCLB, No Child Left Behind Act) requires every state to annually assess and measure every student's progress of skills attained across various subjects. While the overall intent was to track academic performance outcomes and address performances below levels of proficiency, for so many school districts that goal never came to fruition.

The current practice in schools is influenced by time constraints and the need to attend to many other obligations competing for every staff member's limited time.

Generally, the reports are read, information is thoughtfully and carefully distilled, major points of achievement are marveled over, and areas of weakness, which many are hesitant to reveal, tend to make school leaders wince. Then decisions about what to do with all of that information depends on many things. Availability usually influences the first decision. School leaders often decide to pass the reports along to an entire staff during a meeting where volunteers are recruited to join a subcommittee tasked with proposing remedies. It's a rather generic response to a high-stakes report. Graduation rates are impacted by what actions schools take or don't take in response to the assessments.

But what is to be done with the data if guidance is unavailable from very knowledgeable people who can carefully distill reams of data and transform it into workable learning objectives, aligned with specific skills targeted for development, and embedded into every teacher's weekly lesson plan?

Someone Who Can Transform Data into a Student Performance Plan

Under the best of intentions, and if given time and schedules to allow weekly strategy planning sessions, a robust action plan for improving student performances will eventually materialize. Maybe. In the real world of education, most schools do not have the luxury of time to develop those plans. Nor can teaching schedules be altered to accommodate those meetings. Realistically, teachers rarely have time in their busy daily routine to carve out consistent chunks of time to keep track of student daily performances. They take student assignments home and correct the work, write comments, and send invitations to students encouraging them to attend after-school tutorial sessions. The ritual of taking student work home, daily and on weekends, is a testament to how they are willing to use their own personal time. It's just that they don't have the capacity to add more to their already overloaded plates. Many teachers are parents with children; and the responsibilities of attending to the needs of their own families, who so often sacrifice time with mothers and fathers who are teachers and school leaders, is often underappreciated.

So what really does become of those voluminous piles of standardized test reports? After staff consume and mull over the information, which they are hopeful someone took the time to transfer and highlight the most essential areas of concern, most of the time they are then placed in desk draws or on shelves, where they proceed to collect dust. Academic achievement specialists will use the standardized test reports in the manner originally intended: to analyze the results of each student's performance, share findings with each student's teacher, and implement a remedial plan to address learning gaps revealed in the reports.

Including an academic achievement specialist responsible for monitoring student performance outcomes will require an inventory of baseline performance levels. Student learning profile assessments are essential in determining methods of instruction across all content areas and curriculums, which are the key learning resources needed to be aligned in accordance with each student's learning profile. Typically, references to diversification of learning resources are seen as the need to purchase adaptive technology and other resources to assist learning. Based on the needs of students, those resources are an essential addition. It is invaluable to have inclusion specialists available to collaborate with teachers, guide the process of deciding assessments to determine specific types of technology assistance needed, and train teachers on how to use those resources. Diversification of learning resources is key to cultivating classrooms to become exceptional, by making them more inclusive and welcoming of every student, and by ensuring no one gets left behind.

Academic achievement specialists, who are devoted to tracking student performance outcomes, offer teachers techniques for assessing and analyzing data, would co-create a remediation plan with teachers in weekly strategy sessions and institute the routine collection of student work samples to detect and remediate learning gaps on a regular basis. An academic achievement specialist is a critical asset for every school.

For more about the roles and responsibilities of the academic achievement specialist, see page 191 in the appendix.

CHAPTER 12

The Transformative Staffing Model in Action

IN THE PRECEDING CHAPTERS, WE'VE EXPLORED THE TRANSFORMATIVE Staffing Model in depth and seen its potential to bring about the evolutionary growth of first-year teachers into competent educators. By embedding professional support specialists in schools on a full-time basis, we'll help school leaders retain their teaching staff while bringing about positive outcomes that can be measured in all student performance assessments, teacher performance evaluations, graduation rates, and college or post-high-school career tracking.

Another benefit of creating a support system to help teachers and other staff members progress in their professional growth is that it will help reverse the current trajectory of staffing shortages. The habit of cycling in a new teacher to replace the previous unsuccessful teacher will not break the cycle of losing teachers. The answer is to build an effective support framework.

But districts have to avoid the mistake of hiring professional development specialists who are unqualified for the position. Simply wearing a name tag that reads "Professional Development Specialist" is not enough. Unless schools are dedicated to hiring specialists who have the requisite qualifications, the exodus of many more teachers from schools will only continue. It's time for all districts to direct the funding resources necessary for hiring highly qualified staff with a proven record of competency, to support the professional growth and competency of all teachers and school staff.

Another advantage of installing school-based professional development staff is that it will be more effective than the current models used in most districts. Providing daily on-site professional training to improve instructional practices among all staff members is a far better approach than having districts round up teachers once a month—or a few times each school year—to attend professional development seminars. One problem with occasional off-site teacher trainings, as opposed to weekly on-site professional development, is that the out-of-school trainings often address topics or issues unrelated to the actual daily concerns teachers are contending with in their classrooms. The prevalence of topics having little or no relevance to the real professional development needs of teachers reveals a major disconnect between school district leaders and school staff members about the gravity of concerns hindering their school's ability to organizationally operate at the highest education standards. School-based resources will have a higher net gain and rate of return for staff and student performance outcomes.

Another potential downside of off-site teacher trainings is that, despite district expectations, quite often new instructional models seldom carry over into classrooms. With no attention to follow-up, there is little chance that teachers will faithfully implement new models. Without ongoing guidance to ensure that the new material or approach is being used, there is also no way of judging either the degree of effectiveness teachers are having in implementing the new model, or if it is producing the intended outcome. But most importantly, so often the practice of herding teachers to a professional development session for the unveiling of a new model will not result in use of the new model in their classroom, and that is because it has no direct relevance to the skills teachers need to improve the quality of instruction.

Another benefit of in-school support specialists is that they can easily include ancillary staff members who are often charged with the responsibility of educating students. The trend of assigning staff members based on availability, but without ensuring they possess the level of competency required to support students in achieving the highest educational standards, is a waste of what could have been valuable learning time.

But by attending to teachers' professional development needs, we will undoubtedly advance every teacher's level of competency in instruction, which will advance students along their educational learning progression. The successful closure of achievement gaps will bolster students' self-esteem and make them feel exceptionally capable of learning, which will set them up for success in other areas of their lives. This is the long-term goal of the transformative staffing model.

Adding Instructional Efficacy to the Teaching Paradigm

The transformative staffing model is built on the certainty that the *effectiveness* of teacher instruction can be quantifiably measured in student outcomes. But *efficacy* is a more encompassing concept that is influenced by a student's beliefs. Beliefs influence the degree of effort one applies to a task. This distinction is important to understand because self-fulfilling prophecies, where expectations are projected onto students and incorporated as part of the student's own worldview, are present in the foundation of our education system. These predictions (also embodied in stereotypes) influence the degree of effort made by both teachers and students. Biases, including racial, gender, and ethnic, shape expectations, and they can have undue consequences on effectiveness and efficacy in the classroom.

And yet educational efficacy is an absolute necessity if we want every student to succeed in school. Educational efficacy is essential to students' owning responsibility for dedicating the level of effort needed to learn. Educating students goes beyond learning about content. Students need to be taught, and then held accountable for adopting, learning habits that will lead to an effective work ethic. There has never been enough emphasis on how students can appreciate their true learning potential. That is because there has never been enough attention given to the importance of valuing individual learning potential. Valuing one's learning potential requires even being aware of the concept, as well as having access to resources to nurture and develop a student's confidence in their ability to learn. Nurturing self-confidence in their ability to learn requires time and access to resources that will help students cultivate learning skills at every grade level of their 13-year educational journey. Efforts to close learning gaps may start with detection of errors in assignments, tests, or other student work products. But it is important to ascertain whether the errors reflect a misunderstanding of what was taught; for a misunderstanding could be remedied with one or a series of mini lessons to achieve clarification. However, if the errors are due to never having acquired the skills needed for learning, they turn into learning deficits. Deficiencies in learning skills is one of the primary reasons students fail.

Strengthening Instruction by Adding the Why to Prevent Learning Deficiencies

If students do not possess the skills to learn, it greatly hinders their ability to fully comprehend content taught. We usually equate learning deficits with disabilities. Learning disabilities are linked with learning deficits, but the learning deficiencies found in many general education classrooms populated by nondisabled students not only exists, but is widespread. Until we create a process to detect learning gaps and apply remedies—as I proposed in my earlier book, *America's Educational Crossroads*, in the section describing how to close academic achievement gaps—untold numbers of students will have been cycled through an educational system without ever being truly educated.

While there are many categories of specific types of learning skills that can be easily found in a search on the internet, when you are a student in a class and struggling with grasping what is being taught, in that moment an internet search is of little help. A student's education is incomplete if what they are taught includes only the *what*, *where*, *how*, and *when*. The absence of the *why*—and opportunities to test the theory of *why* by having opportunities to generalize and actually apply what's learned to verify how well they understand what has been taught—impacts their ability to retain newly learned concepts and other information. When students have opportunities to use their reasoning skills, it ignites cognitive learning.

Expecting students to make a more rigorous effort has to be preceded by teaching them strategies for learning. Specific examples of what *applying rigorous effort* looks like are also needed. Without teaching students learning strategies at each grade level, tailored to assignments across the spectrum of subjects, their efforts to apply more rigor will be impeded. Maintaining pace with delivery of information, concurrently requiring students to consume and process increased volumes of content presented at rigorously elevated levels, also requires elevation of a higher order of thinking skills.

The current conditions do not include educating students how to learn. Efforts they make, without the benefit of being rewarded with a passing grade, are often a deflating experience. In time, when they conclude there is no point in making an effort, past performance outcomes influence their decision to stop making any effort at all, and they instead rely on luck. And when their reliance on luck does not result in success, they will continue taking a default response where they conclude, "Nothing I do really matters." And then they proceed down the path of apathy.

If we expect students to develop efficacy in learning, it has to derive from first learning how to learn. Math instruction often includes how and what is needed for the process of solving problems. Simply mimicking what and how to do something succeeds in demonstrating a process. Including reasons that explain why provides the connective tissue between the *how*, *what*, and *why*, making learning more likely. It is the *why* that increases the probability of concepts or steps resonating beyond the showing and telling. Understanding the *why* helps strengthen retention because reasons that are clearly understood make content or information more memorable.

Next, we must help students to acquire study habits. Showing them the direct connection between acquiring learning skills and study habits and experiencing their successful performance outcomes is how we prove applying oneself truly works. Key to students' becoming scholars are explicit demonstrations of how learning skills, combined with study habits, improve their ability to sustain focus, prepare for tests, strengthen analytical skills, and distill and process large amounts of information.

The Transformative Staffing Model in Action

One person highly knowledgeable about how effort has a direct influence on performance outcomes in education is Jeff Howard, CEO and chairman of the Efficacy Institute at Harvard University's School of Graduate Studies. I had the privilege of attending one of Jeff's seminars many years ago, and he adroitly demonstrated, by way of a visual model, the direct connection between the level of effort one applies in learning, and the degree of successful outcomes. In other words, the results you get are based on level of effort you put in. However, if students are never provided the tools for learning, they will be frustrated when they do make a sincere effort to apply themselves but do not succeed. This is why it's critical to teach students (and teachers) effective learning skills—instead of simply imploring them to try harder, which just sets them up for failure. The habit of applying effort without knowing what kind of effort to apply is why so many students feel like passengers left behind when the train pulls out of the station.

How do we move beyond ineffective teaching methods in the classroom? Consider this example: A teacher asks, "Does everyone understand this?" But students feel too embarrassed to admit in front of their peers that they do not understand whatever was shared, so they employ learned performative techniques to hide their confusion, masking the truth by vigorously shaking their head to affirm, *Yes, I've got it*. This is a common way students cope, so teachers have to adopt techniques that encourage and make it safe for students to openly and honestly say "I don't understand." That level of trust takes time and layers of peeling away students' apprehensions so they can feel safe to publicly acknowledge they need help. When they submit work that shows learning gaps, despite their having publicly affirmed that they understood the material, it signals the need for teachers to request assistance from a classroom management specialist to help cultivate pathways for openness and honesty in their classrooms. This is also an opportunity for the teacher to check in with the instructional support specialist to find a more effective way to teach this student (and, likely more students who were also afraid to raise their hands).

Clearly, instructional efficacy and learning efficacy are codependent; one impacts the other. If teachers enhance the range of instructional tools while students acquire more rigorous learning skills, we are likely to see incremental improvement. Focusing solely on broadening the range of instructional options, however, is less important than selecting methods of instruction that actually align with, and have proven successful for, the wide spectrum of different learning profiles among students. Teachers who believe in their ability to teach all students because they believe all students are capable of learning are to be commended. But the aspiration of engaging all students in learning, although noble, will not ensure efficacy. Pragmatic, well-thought-out, proven solutions must be introduced into the classroom at the start of each student's educational career and reinforced in each subsequent grade.

Students' efficacy is not predetermined in pre-K or kindergarten or during their elementary school years. However, based on what they experience in the early educational years—for instance, if their learning growth has been impacted by previous failures, over time insecurities will likely continue to grow—their self-esteem and learning efficacy will deflate over time because of their failure. Educational growth begins to stagnate or eventually becomes stunted. When students continually receive the message that they are flawed or prone to failure, behavioral issues often emerge that result in referrals for special education evaluations. With predictable frequency, these students are often placed in special education programs for children with behavioral disruptive disorders, or those who have been diagnosed as fragile or emotionally disturbed. Rarely do we trace the student's maladaptive behavior back to instructional inefficacies.

But for anyone, continual failure will lead to frustration. Rather than assessing student work to find and remedy learning or instructional gaps, the current practice is to assign students Fs and then expect them to dig themselves out of holes that feel like personal failures. If material covered is as mysterious to them by the end of lessons as it was when introduced at the start of the lesson, the initial blocks of self-doubt about one's true ability to learn start stacking up.

This only feeds into the cycle: learning efficacy depends on a student's experiences and influences how much effort they apply. Without intervention, previous failure becomes a self-fulfilling prophecy.

Let's consider an experiment. If we place that same student in a classroom that attends to learning gaps without assigning a failing grade, but instead applies an instructional response as the solution, the student will, with practice, efficaciously develop learning skills. It is not that learning will suddenly become easy; students should expect that learning will be challenging. But the whole trajectory of their career as a student will change when they understand that their teacher will assess errors as a natural part of a process that allows for mistakes. In this new approach, mistakes will be remediated through additional instruction as needed; and in this setting, students will be conditioned to honestly show, without fear of failure, what they know and do not know.

In that environment, teachers will view errors as revelations about what has not yet been learned, and they will have confidence that with a well-constructed remediation plan, the student will certainly be capable of grasping and eventually mastering the content. Were it possible, it would be interesting to compare the learning efficacy of students in school cultures that nurture students through the educational process with safety nets that never allow failure, to schools that hold students responsible for things they did not learn.

Unfortunately, those nurturing schools do not yet exist. Providing teachers with the professional support they need will help to create a learning environment that assures students that they do not need to fear what they do not know—because teaching does not stop when errors are made. Teaching is a continual process where students freely, and without fear, demonstrate what they have learned and what they did not understand. Imagine the freedom and curiosity that will emerge when errors are viewed through an instructional lens, where performance outcomes are assessed without blame. Teaching practices in that kind of school will bring the student through a learning process that allows time, patience, and alternative instruction as needed; a process that will show them that they absolutely possess the capacity to learn. No content, topic, or lesson is insurmountable. This is the kind of education that prepares students to be successful in—and beyond—the classroom.

Part 3: Continuation of Instruction

CHAPTER 13

Ensuring Exceptional Classrooms During Crises

As the world has learned since late 2019, our society at large is much more fragile than we have been prepared for. The COVID-19 pandemic has had an unprecedented impact on the daily lives of millions of people and has disrupted the routines that our lives are built on: school, work, family, and community. While the pandemic's effects were global, individual communities have increasingly faced other threats that disrupt everyday lives, such as climate disasters, mass violence, and school violence. Solving these complex problems is beyond the scope of this book. But in order to cultivate exceptional classrooms so that our students can excel, we must prepare for these and similar events. That is why I'm advocating for a national Continuation of Education Plan (CEP) that will be customized and implemented at the local level. Disaster preparedness experts, infrastructure specialists, policymakers, parent groups, and local educators will work together to develop this plan. It will have enough flexibility to adapt to changing needs, as well as a strong mandate, with accountability measures built in, so that we can rely on its being there when we need it. But before we explore the CEP, let's review how being unprepared for COVID has impacted our students and communities.

Education in the Time of COVID: The Domino Effect of School Closures During the Pandemic

As difficult as the COVID-19 pandemic was for everyone, children in low-income communities were especially impacted—and the damage is ongoing because of the months of instruction they missed out on. Many of these students' adult family members were labeled "essential" workers and had no say in whether or not they wanted to work under very scary health conditions. Initially, no vaccines were available, and these workers had to work in conditions that placed them and their families at great risk of being infected by a rampant virus that was not yet understood. Months passed before adequate protective measures were enacted, and personal protective equipment was not readily available—even to workers at the highest risk.

While many workers in higher income brackets were able to work from home during the pandemic, America's poorest class of citizens were among the first to be exposed to the virus, hospitalized, and intubated on ventilators, which too often proved to be an insufficient lifesaving measure. Because COVID-19 was a new virus, it took time for scientists to understand the means of transmission and the best ways to treat patients. But the problem was compounded by government leaders' failure to take action. As it became clear that many of the most vulnerable populations were minorities in poor communities, the government's lack of urgency was just one of many signs indicating racism was behind a quiet policy that made collateral damage acceptable.

In this environment, "essential" working parents generally had no choice about going to work—they were needed to keep the country functioning, and they generally lacked savings to be able to weather the pandemic. Working parents of children born into poverty were often unable to afford the technology that remote learning relies on, and so they were forced to forfeit their child's education. For so many parents, the discontinuation of their child's education in school led to the realization that school meals were an essential part of their family life. But food wasn't the only form of starvation kids in poor communities had to learn to live with during the remote learning.

Closures of day care and after-school programs meant essential workers had no supervised care for their children while they were at work. Even if day care was available, many were not able to afford it. So parents who desperately needed their incomes had to risk leaving their children alone—and starving for attention, food, education, and friends or some form of companionship. For the families of "essential" workers, the dominoes just kept falling.

For families who did have access to the tools for remote learning, the pandemic still presented an unprecedented challenge: parents became frustrated with the responsibility of being surrogate teachers. First of all, parents were unprepared and did not know what was expected of them. Then, when it became apparent that they were needed to participate on a higher level than they expected, or contrary to the minimal role they were originally led to believe they would have in remote learning, things became untenable. Families were subjected to stress tests due to changes in routines, roles, and at times collective frustration. Students wanted their parents to remain in the parental role. But when the crossover occurred and parents were imploring teachers to help them make their kid sign in, participate, and remain seated at their computers for the entirety of each session, the role reversal gave parents a glimpse of how demanding teaching can be. But in fairness to parents, schools have a way of conditioning and acclimating students to environments that do not have the distractions of a bed, television, and other electronic devices in the same room where learning is expected to take place. Nor are there refrigerators next door for frequent snack runs, or a family pet available for show-and-tells to disrupt lessons.

Parents may have also rediscovered their own long-forgotten challenges with schooling. In addition, core subjects have changed dramatically since the time adult parents attended elementary, middle, and high school. Much of parents' resistance was related to fearing the unknown, and then being embarrassed by a feeling of being an inadequate surrogate teacher. But teachers know about being a surrogate. They are often relegated to step into the role of emotional surrogate parents during school hours. Knowing that, however, does not diminish parents' rights to feel a bit daunted and at times downright overwhelmed. They and their children had never encountered such unimaginable circumstances.

For many families, remote learning was their first introduction to instruction on the Zoom platform, and the process of having to become familiar with a new tool on the spur of the moment likely caused some aggravation. But soon parents discovered that their physical presence was needed to monitor Zoom instruction, and their responsibilities shifted from those of a parent to those of a study hall monitor. Parents who were essential workers faced an even more difficult situation because they often had to leave their children at home and merely hope they would be okay— and possibly participate in Zoom instructional sessions.

In some families, frustration levels brought about mutual decisions, but for different reasons: both parent and child decided to abandon remote instruction sessions. Ultimately, the tension created by the growing stress brought on by the persistent resistance of some children in homes became a turning point. Depending upon how children and parents experienced remote learning, for many families it changed minds about education being a priority. That became evident when online attendance started to decline. The absenteeism likely began to spike exponentially when parents decided they were not going to fill in as substitutes for teachers. Many parents recognized that they were never trained to teach and resented the assumption that they could, would, and should take on that responsibility.

Parents and students both wanted to get back to in-school learning, with one very important caveat for most parents: "Not until I know it's safe for my child to attend school in person." Unfortunately, the country did not have a uniform approach or a universal standard for enacting safety measures in schools, which led to more uncertainty, higher risk of infection, and confusion when schools would briefly reopen before having to abruptly close once again.

As if remote learning were not complicated enough, one cannot help wondering what the lives of teachers with children were like: having to balance providing instruction while supporting their own children with remote learning.

Continuation of Education Plan

As both COVID and smaller, more localized crises have demonstrated, in order to safeguard student learning and well-being, our education system needs to prepare students for the continuation of education under a variety of potential circumstances. To do this, we must develop a Continuation of Education Plan (CEP) that explicitly states how schools will continue student education during unexpected and disruptive circumstances—whether pandemics, extreme weather events, or school violence and mass violence. By making well-informed plans in advance, we can ensure the continuity of education for all students. Attempts to respond to any crisis while in the midst of contending with the crisis is unacceptable.

Among the many lessons learned during the pandemic is the need for a comprehensive plan that is produced in advance and adequately designed to anticipate what alternative education sites, resources, and safety protocols will be needed to enable education to continue under a variety of potentially challenging circumstances. In addition to preparing for alternative sites and resources, all schools must include transportability plans for daily school resources to follow teachers and students to alternative education sites. A CEP allows a student's education to proceed along a continuum of previously planned steps. As the word *continuum* implies, providing a clearly stated model in advance signals the district and their school staff's intention to maintain the continuation of education regardless of circumstances. We just have to design a comprehensive plan today to prepare for future catastrophic events that may require distance learning . . . again.

If we build a CEP now, then disseminate it to families throughout every community, it could go a long way toward allaying fears and apprehensions related to future health crises. We are generally conditioned to fear the unknown. So why not at least acknowledge all of the numerous gaps we have been made aware of and build models to help us prepare for those circumstances, in advance, so we can turn down our fear barometers and not sit in a state of terror in anticipation of "the next one"? Our children look to adults in their day-to-day lives for assurances of how to deal with future catastrophic events like COVID. If they see adults living in fear while waiting for the next time, they are likely to interpret our adult anguish as a signal that translates into a feeling of being unprotected and at the mercy of whatever may come in their future. We cannot allow them to see the role of protectors solely on movie and TV screens in the form of heroes with superpowers. Those characters are intended to be a source of entertainment. COVID has taught us that the best form of getting through, and not escaping from, the real-world uncertainties is to prepare for those uncertainties.

Education cannot and should not take on any form of negative connotation for kids. But if, instead of doing nothing but stew about what we all just experienced, we and our government take proactive measures to plan for similar circumstances, we could prevent a recurrence of the same outcomes. Why should students inherit a lasting memory of all of the things related to education that COVID took away from them? The incentive for the public's supporting a government plan of safety measures for potential future pandemics could best be couched in helping the public recall the experiences of their children, who had to participate virtually in graduations and other socially rewarding and traditionally in-person events students generally look forward to in schools. Does the public really want virtual events to become the new norm? The Continuation of Education Plan solely addresses a way to maintain our ability to not disrupt a student's education, but some creative people will have to imagine and develop a Continuation of School Events Plan to address alternative ways to preserve the momentous occasions that matter to every student's social, emotional, mental, and developmental well-being.

For many years, school buildings have been the hub of our education systems; they have been where learning takes place. But the pandemic introduced us to the need to view learning through a broader lens. If we broaden the concept of cultivating exceptional classrooms to include any and all locations used to deliver quality instruction to produce high-performance outcomes, then *where* students are educated will not be restricted to schools.

Prior to COVID, some urban school districts explored ways to expand education platforms to allow mobility and transportability of education for high school students interested in taking courses to recover credits. Districts invested in providing students opportunities to graduate through distance learning because they wanted to prevent students from dropping out or to reinvest those who had already left but were a few credits shy of earning a diploma. Discovering the rates of success colleges and universities were having using online courses, high schools wanted to replicate the pattern of success. In districts that rolled-out online programs, similar to students enrolled in college, the model became a much-preferred route to obtaining a diploma. Within a few years after high schools launched online courses, graduation rates increased and dropout rates began to decline. Technology provided the link and opportunity needed to create online courses for young adults to pursue and successfully complete college-degree programs. The progression of online programs in high schools became popular.

As kinks occurred, school districts discovered the independent learning model was not a suitable fit for every student. For some, as the work became increasingly rigorous, teacher assistance was needed. Students who were inadequately prepared for self-instruction also encountered challenges. Despite those difficulties, high schools that invested in online courses as an option during in-person learning were among the most prepared when schools transitioned to remote learning.

These experiences have shaped my recommendations for the Continuation of Education Plan, which should prepare students, families, teachers, and communities to replicate an exceptional learning environment, no matter where the learning is taking place. We must first cultivate exceptional classrooms for all students and then ensure access to that high level of education, regardless of the crises that might arise. We need to take these specific steps to make sure quality education is accessible for all students—even during regional and national emergencies or hardships:

- Seamlessly build technology into our everyday classroom instruction so that it becomes a natural part of each student's learning routine.

- Create a network of satellite classrooms embedded in each community so that students can have safe locations closer to home that allow for continued social contact while maintaining social distancing.

- Improve the internet infrastructure so that no home is without internet access.

- Ensure the continuation of support by professional development specialists so that the teacher support infrastructure remains intact and effective.

In short, we need to build redundant methods of providing instruction into our education system and create a truly "transportable" education system to ensure that every student has effective and equitable access to quality education.

Lessons Learned About the Importance of Technology in the Classroom

At the start of the pandemic, many students, parents, and even teachers had not heard of instruction via remote at-home learning or hybrid-education models. One way to mitigate most of the apprehension and fear of remote learning is to teach students how to do tasks remotely while in school. Embedding a remote-learning lesson into the routine of each student's daily class schedule while attending school will reduce, if not totally eliminate, the need for a freakout-odometer when districts announce the need for school closings and remote learning. But the absolute best approach to preparing students is to also prepare their families. The Open House event is a great place to inform parents about opportunities for them to sign up for hands-on informational sessions about remote learning—what it is and how it works—and then put parents through a virtual class lesson to allow them to become acclimated.

In-school orientations should be followed with weekly live-streamed lessons on digital platforms like Zoom, and other digital sources to be used for remote instruction. Allowing students continued access to hands-on remote learning tools and instructional methods on digital platforms while in school will broaden their instruction and learning comfort zone. Students' and teachers' familiarizing themselves with what the actual education process will look like and how to use those resources in advance will also make for smoother transitions from schools to hybrid or other remote locations. Orientations should also include information related to expectations for attendance, the continued practice of providing additional instructional support to address learning gaps, and the performance evaluation process. Students and families should also be made aware of how daily and weekly class work will be assigned.

Conditioning students in how they will be expected to socially conduct themselves while in remote learning settings is also important. While many of the social interactions that occur daily in class can be carried over from healthy and respectful social habits developed in class, expect those boundaries to be tested. As is so often the case when introducing students to new experiences, even familiar and well-known guardrails will be tested under foreign conditions. Time to get acclimated will be needed, but being transparent, in advance, about what is non-negotiable during the transition and throughout the period of remote instruction will shorten the time needed to become acclimated.

The quality of instruction while attending school in person will have a great deal of carryover effect in other locations. How students experience education while in school is essential to the level of credibility they will assign to their education when they are outside of traditional classroom settings. The importance of viewing our system through a lens focused on how students experience education, instead of assessing and grading their academic performance or determining level of testing aptitude on standardized tests, came into greater focus during remote learning. Once students began receiving instruction beyond the brick-and-mortar educational facilities, whatever educational frustrations they had experienced while in school were magnified in many different forms during the time students were assigned to home instruction. The list of ways students experienced social, emotional, mental, and physical frustration, which for many turned into illness, is far too long and, in all honesty, too sad to share. Being deprived of much-needed social interactions with peers reveals a need to think of innovative ways students can socially interact while social distancing. It may be beneficial to survey students about what they would recommend for socially engaging activities to strengthen class cohesion. It will be difficult replicating social interactions and games students shared during recess, or friendships that had an opportunity to blossom in the cafeteria, but we must take what we learned about the consequences of being socially deprived from peers as a sign to never neglect other areas of importance to students. Continued Education Plans (CEPs) have to include the holistic needs of students. Exploring ways for students to continue the totality of in-school experiences during virtual learning may seem next to impossible. But often when we endeavor to find ways to make what initially seems impossible possible, it means we just have not figured out a way to do something . . . yet.

What is absolutely certain is our ability to acclimate students to the variety of educational resources that will be made available remotely by merging them with instruction during in-person learning. Familiarity with tools and resources prior to circumstances where they will be utilized expands students' level of comfort and will make transitions more seamless.

Satellite Classroom Networks

Given the enormity of the recent national health crisis, we may have to foresee a future where education can no longer be available solely within one physical structure. A health pandemic on the scale of COVID-19, and concerns about subsequent variants, will dictate the terms of safety measures and protocols needed to support maximum protection of everyone. Social distancing for schools cannot and should not always result in confining students to their homes for remote instruction. But how do we achieve social distancing and reduce the size of student populations in classrooms initially designed for larger populations?

The ability to maintain quality instruction is a priority. One way to do this is to create an intermediate tier between in-school learning and fully remote in-home learning: the satellite classroom network. Because many schools are not physically able to accommodate social distancing protocols for the large student populations they serve, I recommend imagining ways to configure a network of technology-ready satellite classrooms inside of organizations throughout every neighborhood. Many students live within walking distance of public libraries, Boys and Girls Clubs, community centers, faith-based organizations, and a variety of other spaces that can be converted into remote learning centers. Each network of satellite classrooms would be linked to a neighborhood school, which, in addition to remaining open and available to a small population of students, would also serve as the main hub of oversight and remain responsible for the continuation of every student's education. Districts would need to work with schools to help facilitate distribution of all school supplies, assign students, teachers, and staff to each remote learning classroom, and monitor daily operations during school hours. This hybrid version of remote learning would enable education to continue, reduce the need for parents to miss work, and prevent the destabilization of students' social and emotional well-being.

The goal is to develop digitally accessible instructional networks to accommodate every student in every neighborhood, so when schools shutter their doors, it does not result in the shuttering of any student's education. In situations where social distancing requires smaller student populations, the classrooms inside schools should remain available during remote instruction. Downsizing the number of students in every class should not preclude schools from continuing to operate. Rather, not operating at full student capacity due to social distancing means schools have to reconfigure classrooms and other spaces to safely accommodate smaller groups of students. Students with special needs should receive the highest priority for continuing their education at their schools. Schools are equipped with the variety of services and equipment needed to meet the educational needs of their special education population. Therefore, districts should allow schools to retain those students instead of distributing them to other locations. While almost all students assigned to an alternative satellite classroom will need time to adjust, or may find the experience challenging, the vulnerability is greater for people with disabilities. There is no need to further impede their education by moving them to other sites if it can be avoided.

Schools' seating capacity under social distancing protocols should be used to determine if more satellite classroom sites are needed. The priority would be to ensure that there is enough seating capacity for all students to participate in remote instruction delivered at satellite classrooms throughout their neighborhood. If every neighborhood had access to internet-equipped community organizations capable of accommodating remote learning, city planners could designate satellite classroom sites to schools right now.

But the full process of converting spaces into mini-satellite classrooms takes time. Locating the spaces is only the first step. In addition to making sure each satellite classroom has proper ventilation, is safe, and has functioning internet access, every location should also have a stockpile of basic protective gear, first-aid supplies, and protocols for entry and egress, as well as contact tracing, quarantine steps, and the like. Because these satellite locations will be called into use during crises, it's critical that they have a range of supplies on hand and a uniform operational plan so they can handle a diverse range of situations. Creating satellite classrooms might seem like an ambitious plan, but when we consider that our communities have the resources to wire entire neighborhoods to accommodate traffic lights and security cameras on almost every block, it seems natural to assume we also possess the means to expand the current digital infrastructure to accommodate the continuation of education.

To develop a comprehensive blueprint for the satellite classroom network, cities will need to mobilize communities' members across a range of interests and specialties. All partners need to be made fully aware of the model's goals; identify spaces capable of being converted on short notice into learning centers within a school's radius, and then create a plan to prepare these spaces to function as satellite classrooms in order to prevent the loss of valuable learning time. By designing this local network, schools will be better able to respond to emergencies without throwing the entire educational system (and students' lives) into chaos and turmoil. Collaboration among organization leaders willing to make space available for satellite classrooms will need assurances, and a drafted plan for each school will maintain full authority and responsibility for the resumption of education when students are assigned to their locations for the duration of emergencies.

As communities work together to implement the satellite classroom network, they will probably have to face infrastructure issues that have gone unaddressed for years, in addition to the need to retrofit buildings for student populations. For example, many school buildings do not accommodate students and staff who need more mobility options, but these needs must be addressed—in both permanent school buildings and satellite classrooms. Likewise, community buildings might need to designate one or two current adult bathrooms to be retrofitted to accommodate elementary-age children by installing shorter toilets and sinks. Shorter water fountains should also be considered.

The subject of water consumption brings to mind broader health and safety concerns emerging in findings impacting the education of generations of students. Research has shown evidence of severe learning deficiencies among students who drink lead-contaminated water transferred into their homes and schools through outdated pipelines. Contaminated pipelines have received the attention of our federal government. Unfortunately, the amount of attention given is insufficient compared to the magnitude of the problem. Despite measures taken by the Centers for Disease Control (CDC) and other prevention efforts to reassure the public of reduced levels of lead in tap water, the list of ways lead can still enter our drinking water remains quite extensive and worrisome. In a CDC report describing "Steps taken under requirements of the 1986 and 1996 amendments to the Safe Drinking Water Act and the U.S. Environmental Protection Agency's (EPA's) Lead and Copper Rule," I did not find the outcome of those steps taken to be highly persuasive. In fact, in the very same report, the CDC shared a detailed list of contributing factors that only serve to undermine the effect of those measures; statements like, "Even so, lead in water can come from a home with lead service lines that connect the home to the main water line" ("Lead in Drinking Water, Sources of Lead," CDC.gov). Most homes, schools and other public buildings are very likely connected to main water lines. The presence of lead in pipelines carrying acidic chemicals, and other unhealthy minerals that contaminate water, into schools and homes has compelled some communities to start replacing unsafe pipelines.

Alarms started sounding across rural and urban communities plagued by numerous health concerns directly linked to the consumption of highly contaminated water flowing through corrosive and decayed lead pipes. While not always brought to the public's attention, communities that have already invested or are currently investing in overhauling their entire water pipeline system are not only addressing health concerns, they are also well aware that the water passing through contaminated lead pipes has led to delays or declining cognitive development growth of children and youth of all ages. The dramatic increase in students' being diagnosed with learning disabilities, many of which will follow a large number of children and teens throughout their lifetimes, is an enormous challenge facing families and our public education system. Awareness of the broad scope and enormously large scale of this problem has not received the high level of attention it deserves. But since we are examining factors that influence our ability to educate students, we clearly need to build future education facilities with newly installed safe water lines. In addition to new water lines, our education system needs to design programs to meet the educational needs of young populations previously exposed to poisonous lead contaminants in our water system.

Anticipation of Satellite Classroom Concerns

While there are many complex layers involved in developing an effective satellite classroom network, it's critical to keep the focus on students and how this arrangement must serve their needs in order to be considered successful. Let's first revisit pragmatic steps to quell the anxiety of students and their families. Start with revealing what the plans are for continuing education in hybrid and remote-learning centers. As previously discussed, a Continuation of Education Plan is a model designed to guide school staff, students, and families through the process of transitioning education from schools to other locations in each school's surrounding community. The plan is intended to support a seamless transition from schools during times of relocation.

Assurances of a smooth transition to a hybrid model of a remote-learning education plan, instead of remote-learning from home full time, will be comforting news to everyone. When informed in advance about the plans, many students and family members will feel a sense of assurance. Remember, the network of satellite classrooms is an effective contingency plan because it is designed to offset the fear of future situations like the COVID pandemic. At best, knowing that well-prepared plans exist to respond to those *break glass* moments will help everyone remain calmer and hopefully be a little less afraid.

At the start of each school year, a list should be prepared of every school's network of community satellite classroom partners to serve as alternative learning sites. This list should then be distributed to every teacher, who should then be informed of where their class of 20-plus students will be spread out and assigned in smaller groups of eight or fewer students. Facilities that can accommodate an entire student population divided into three separate spaces would enable the teacher to oversee instruction in one facility. If we want this model to work, it has to be designed in a way that will give it a chance to work. But admittedly, even this is an imperfect model that may ultimately require more staffing. If hiring additional staff and substitute teachers is needed to ensure every smaller class is provided a full time, qualified instructor, districts should plan accordingly.

A system of preplanned relocation of classrooms for teachers and students has to be shared with families in advance. And like the remote and hybrid learning orientation plan, students should have time to adjust to the satellite classrooms too. Even if there never comes a time where they will need to be relocated, it would still be beneficial to plan a field trip to the alternative site and experience learning in those locations, just as a precaution. Orienting everyone by visiting hybrid and remote learning classrooms in advance may elevate assurances of being well prepared.

Transitions under any circumstances can be a challenging experience. Some of those challenges can be significantly reduced by preparing for transitions while being transparent and candid about what those changes will entail. Preparing parents and students in advance for any contingency is needed. So too is the need to pay particular attention to helping students prepare for detaching from their schools. That is important because, for the majority of students, the only physical structure they have ever associated with their education is their school. The detachment from a physical structure of the magnitude of importance schools carry is an emotional, psychological, mental, and physical process. Preparing for the need to transition from schools to other locations to continue their education will be experienced differently; some students possess the ability to "go with the flow" and adapt quickly, whereas others are highly fragile individuals. As funny as it may sound, teachers may have to think creatively about what artifacts, like photos of the school and classroom, students can take with them as reminders of where they will one day return to. Visual and tangible items that mean something to students can strengthen a student's comfort level during the transition period. Visual and tangible artifacts may help emotionally anchor students who may benefit from periodically looking at the artifacts to remind them to remain aspirational about returning to their school. Visiting classroom satellite sites will also help students to anticipate where they will be transitioning to. But if schools neglect the need to also orient students, while in school, about the instructional resources for remote learning at other sites, it will be a missed opportunity to lessen anxiety levels when the time does come to relocate.

Preparing Students for Satellite Classrooms and Remote Learning

Lack of availability of internet bandwidth is a serious problem—and one of the main obstacles that prevents poor students from being able to continue their education via remote learning. Ideally, every home in America should have access to adequate bandwidth. But, if internet cannot be provided to every home, then community leaders and politicians need to work with tech companies to create networks of digitally accessible communities, where at a minimum internet is installed in federal- and state-funded locations like public libraries and any organization that applies for and receives federal funding.

Leaders should follow the lead of governors and mayors in exploring partnerships with private industry and corporations to financially support citywide installation of bandwidth access in every community in cities.

The World Economic Forum showed a few examples of successful outcomes of partnerships between community leaders and tech-based private corporations. New York City is a prime example of what is possible to bring digital connectivity to communities without access to bandwidth resources. According to the 2018 report, "A Quarter of Urban Americans Don't Have Broadband Access. Here's Why" (WeForum.org), "New York Mayor Bill de Blasio launched the OneNYC initiative aimed at providing every resident and business in New York with access to adequate and affordable broadband by 2025. OneNYC also helped provide free Wi-Fi to around 3,500 residents, and offered dedicated support for senior citizens as well as for young people and their families." Later in the report, it was stated that the decision to provide access to digital resources for a higher number of citizens in New York continued with the launch of another project, LinkNYC (LynkNYC.com). "[The] LinkNYC project included repurposing New York's payphone infrastructure with free Wi-Fi, targeting at least 7,500 payphone kiosks to be installed in the city by 2025, providing superfast broadband for residents."

Creative minds should think of incentives to entice corporate leaders to consider contributing to the development of community-based internet-access installation projects throughout the city. Those same companies could be asked to donate open spaces in their facilities to support satellite classrooms. In this modern environment, internet access is more than a luxury; blanketing entire communities with digital access will serve as a firewall to protect our education system.

Under ideal conditions, if a variety of other education-technology platforms had been introduced to students prior to COVID, students might have been better prepared to continue with their education during the remote-school phase—with one exception. Those ideal conditions would have required that students have access to the same level of bandwidth at home as that available inside of schools. Consequently, even when schools distributed laptops in poor neighborhoods, the students were at a disadvantage because they didn't have internet services. It was especially disheartening for students who did receive computers but were unable to use them.

It is estimated that well over 50% of students in poor communities lost connectivity with their education during the remote-learning period. The percentage of students disconnected from their education makes it abundantly clear that the missing links in our education system are not just limited to the professional needs of school staff. Capacity in accessing technology is another missing link that is critical to our education delivery system. We now know the difference between capacity and possessing the economic resources to bring the "capacity" of technology into people's residences. Those unable to afford the convenience and full "capacity" of modern technology were subjected to a series of consequences where, similar to falling dominos, one area had a negative effect on numerous others.

In order to provide effective instruction and learning environments along the full spectrum—from in-school learning to satellite classrooms to remote in-home learning—each community and home needs affordable access to adequate internet. As a nation, we have the ability to bring these resources to bear on behalf of all students—if we make it a priority.

Mobility of New Professional Development Resources

The goal for any Continuation of Education Plan is that it must be capable of resuming students' education seamlessly and at the highest level of quality. Even under the unique conditions of remote learning, we cannot pause education. For this reason, each school's professional development specialist will be trained to adapt to remote learning. Their primary responsibility will continue to be to function as a professional safety net for teachers, but they will also expand their efforts as necessary, for example, to help motivate students to participate in online learning and to provide support for parents of children who refuse to log in to classes. When remote learning occurs in students' homes, parents should have direct access to specialists. Having a well-thought-out CEP allows schools to prepare in advance for what everyone now knows to expect, which will reduce teachers' and family members' apprehension during remote learning. Retaining availability of all resources can benefit every teacher's comfort level with carrying out their responsibilities to the best of their ability under any unique circumstances.

The following is a list of some ways schools can mobilize and transfer resources from primary school buildings to remote learning settings.

- As much as possible, have remote learning mimic normal routines used in schools.
- Teachers should work in collaboration with professional support specialists to develop plans to transfer classroom routines and other norms to hybrid and remote-learning settings, including remote learning from home.
- School leaders, professional specialists, and other staff members should work with teachers to prepare classroom-specific (taking into consideration the diverse needs of students assigned to each class) remote-learning tool kits that inform all families, at the start of each school year, of educational services planned to support the continuation of education. Tool kits will include a copy of the

Continuation of Education Plan, lists of instructional resources, class management support, curriculum, and content planning, as well as tech-support allocation to students and parents. Each resource will include the names, positions, and contact information of staff members and specialists responsible for instruction, content, technology support, classroom management support (related to attendance, student participation, and performance expectations), and academic-achievement monitoring.

- Identify policies and instructional practices used in school that can be replicated for remote learning from satellite classrooms or homes.

- Prepare students and parents about modifications being made as needed.

- Make all families and residents throughout the community aware that schools are the hub for each network of satellite classrooms around the community.

- Assemble a parent/teacher group to openly discuss what went wrong in the COVID remote-learning period (particularly related to technology glitches, and the lack of adequate resources for students who don't own computers and have no access to the internet at home). Request that the assembled participants design a plan that lists areas in which they would like to receive support, where they can share and expect responses for concerns and complaints, identify who is in charge of what (i.e., the chain of command during hybrid and remote learning in satellite classroom learning centers), schedule parent-teacher-specialist check-ins, and address other safety-net areas of concern.

- Create a Social Activities Planning Committee to support the bonding of the entire student population with friends and peers. Explore events to elevate spirits, bring about joy, and allow students to excitedly anticipate in ways they used to for school proms, graduations, and other special events.

Just as teachers, families, and students will need to adjust their expectations and approaches to instruction/learning, the professional development specialists will need to shift their focus at times. Many students from different populations will face crisis-related hurdles in and outside of the classroom. In some cases, discrimination and bias might take a different form in remote-learning situations than it does in in-person education, so inclusion specialists will need to adapt their methods to make sure all students have access to the level of teaching they need. Very little is said about the human interactions between students and teachers, but just as establishing a rapport with every student when physically present in school is essential for cultivating a social connection while in person, such rapport is necessary for supporting students' academic performance under remote-learning conditions. Specialists must have contingency plans for training educators to develop rapport-building skills, even when students are physically unable to attend school.

Delivering Quality Education Across All Platforms

Let's just start by stating what many of us already know. If substandard education was what was occurring during in-school learning, what do we imagine followed students home when their schools were shut down? What about students who had no access to digital learning because their families could not afford the cost of installing the needed technology?

Public schooling in poor communities isn't just lagging behind compared to public education in economically wealthier neighborhoods. The absence of modern technological resources in poor communities makes it almost impossible for students to access quality education even in remote and remote-hybrid scenarios.

As explained in Parts 1 and 2 of this book, the first step in cultivating exceptional classrooms is to improve the quality of education delivered inside of schools through the use of professional development specialists. These links, unmasked and described in Part 2, as well as in the appendix, must continue to be accessible for teachers and students during the Continuation of Education Plan, or CEP. The goal is to create a seamless thread that transitions all school resources from the in-school environment to satellite classrooms to in-home remote schooling. It is imperative to maintain the links between specialists and teachers across all education and learning platforms. In other words, wherever teachers and students go, so will the professional development specialists. Beyond that, school districts need to share with the public—especially with teachers and families—how they intend to maintain the responsibility of educating students, regardless of the circumstances. For the CEP to succeed—and for the quality of education not to suffer during crises—the plan must be practical, feasible, and enforceable—and it must be communicated clearly to all stakeholders.

It may be wishful thinking to imagine that expanding internet access and creating a durable, portable education system, bolstered by professional development specialists, would be enough to raise communities out of poverty. But I think we have to expand our understanding of other forms of bandwidths to include *awareness* and *compassion*. Developing broader bandwidths of awareness and compassion could jumpstart a movement about the importance of understanding the necessity and benefits of digital bandwidth in currently neglected urban and rural communities.

Successfully closing bandwidth gaps will eventually reduce the digital divide and eventually disrupt the continuation of a status quo that has not worked for generations of students. Those without digital access to education, and many other resources requiring internet access, will remain living in poverty. Being subjected to ongoing inequitable standards, such as technology resources, devalues their lives and their opportunities to show their true academic potential. Neglecting their needs for assistance to educationally progress in order to improve their future social status impedes their ability to continue ascending up economic and social ladders in their futures. Over time, they will inherit the permanent status of those unfortunate to have been born poor and then left to flounder in impoverished conditions.

CHAPTER 14

Emotional/Mental Health and the Continuation of Instruction

As a nation, we've learned much about ourselves, our government, and our neighbors through the COVID-19 pandemic. We can't undo the mistakes of our recent past, but we, as an extended community, can learn from them. Learning from the pandemic can help us prepare for the next one—or the next mudslide, hurricane, uncontrolled forest fire, or domestic terrorist attack. Weather-related catastrophes that destroy whole communities will make any efforts to continue education almost impossible. However, we are a recovery-minded country. Therefore, while our control of outside forces might be limited, taking action to improve and preserve education for students from all communities is well within our power—and it is our responsibility.

Not only is transitioning from hair-on-fire crisis mode to a calm, collected, and rational mode possible, but our children are looking to us, as adults, to be the role models. When children see adults remaining level-headed and committed to rationally responding to circumstances that frighten even us, it can be a source of comfort and help them endure situations with less internalized trauma. All we can do under the harshest circumstances is to try to recognize the existence of, and maintain the resolve to stay with, to the best of our human ability, whatever effort is required to mitigate any potential long- or short-term dangers.

Preventing Health Insecurity Gaps

To reverse our newest insecurity gap, we need to ensure that our country relies on a science-based, responsive, judicious, and equitable public health policy. During COVID, mixed signals, politically motivated health protocols, and a profound lack of leadership left parents in a great deal of consternation and confusion about whether or not to send their children to school.

When government assurances lack transparency and accuracy, or worse, their messages of reassurance are understandably met with resistance—particularly when direct questions are met with answers that sound like obfuscation—those moments are what contribute to increased concerns and the widening of health insecurity gaps. When those in positions of authority make claims that run contrary to evidence, the gaps become further reasons for mistrust. Those responsible for allaying public concerns have to start with being truthful. As discussed in previous chapters, we cannot be subjected to information or actions that continue to erode our trust in our education system. No one should be surprised when the public demands that all communication be accurate and verifiable by trusted sources.

While the author would respectfully defer to those far more knowledgeable about the topic of virus safety tips, it is worth recommending that school districts develop, in conjunction with health care experts and members of the medical-science community, a scientifically backed Health Assurance Plan that provides unbiased, apolitical best practices that can be implemented in a variety of community health crises. Closing health insecurity gaps is possible when communities are able to rely on being fully informed about facts from reliable sources.

A New Model of Counseling

During the pandemic, when schools did finally reopen, we did not recognize just how badly wounded—emotionally, psychologically, and mentally—students were upon their return. Many of those who survived the pandemic are in desperate need of counseling. But the current counseling practices available in schools are insufficient to address the range of critical needs that students brought back to school with them. And this is why we need a new counseling model.

We recently learned that drastic times do call for drastic measures. And like everything else, drastic events have thrust schools into an entirely different terrain, completely untethering them from their responsibility of solely providing education. Schools are communal settings and important anchors for students and families across all communities in our country. School closings removed a familiar and much-relied-upon routine that played a significant part in making other daily routines, like going to work, possible. The absence of schools in our daily lives deepened everyone's appreciation for schools. So many programs—ranging from meals, to sports, clubs, and social and other community events—are lifelines benefiting students, families, and local organizations that partner with schools to sponsor events. Closing schools became the equivalent of shuttering the most prominent social hub in every neighborhood. Discovering just how much schools are one of those institutions that serve as anchors in every community makes it even more understandable why we still haven't fully recovered from being without them, even after they reopened. The duration of time we were without this valued resource has left an emotional scar.

The onset of the pandemic, driven by a rapidly spreading, highly contagious, and deadly virus, was unlike any other national and global event experienced in America in recent memory. It didn't just take the lives of loved ones, it did so at a dizzying pace—leaving us unable to keep up with the level of contagion, especially since during the initial months no vaccines, only mistruths, were made available to combat the virus.

While the absence of education over an extended period widened academic achievement gaps, which were already a concern prior to school closings, students in poor communities suffered both education and food insecurity—and often had to spend time home without the security and comfort of a responsible adult. Over time, families recognized the role schools also played in the social, emotional, and developmental well-being of children, teens, and young adults, who were now unable to attend school and college. Students faced time away from others, while enduring the loss of those who died . . . and not being able to say their goodbyes in person, give and receive hugs, or hold one another just one more time.

Empty schools seemed to create an emptiness felt by untold numbers of students. Being without access to friends and peers induced feelings of isolation for many kids and teens. Over time, their descriptions of how it felt being cooped up inside of their homes, learning remotely without social outlets for so long, were warning signs of possible mental illness and depression.

We are fairly used to events that shake our nation to the core, but generally, after the initial and terrifying experience, we've been able—through grace, community vigils, ceremonies, prayers, and outreach to those most affected—to work our way through the trauma, and we then resume our normal lives. But the arrival of COVID-19, a pandemic that rolled through communities at high rates and took the lives of so many people with minimal warning, was jarring for everyone. COVID not only demanded our full attention for a prolonged period, but it continues to do so. And it is because of the dimensions—including the global scale—of this crisis that we will not have the luxury of relying on a definitive timeline where we can eventually say, "Finally, we can pick up the pieces and move on from that tragedy."

As resilient as students are in masking their true emotions, expecting them to seamlessly transition back to school and a different version of life is unfair. They may be quietly enduring ongoing pain and still suffering on the inside, but we cannot allow them to bear that burden alone. Just because we cannot see it does not mean the deep wounds are no longer present. The current levels of fragility related to so much tragedy experienced over the past several years should compel us to reassess levels and types of counseling needed for all people, but especially students.

But how do we accomplish this? For a moment, let's step back and view the solutions we've explored so far: First, by embedding professional development specialists in every school, we can focus on perfecting instructional systems while students are attending school for in-person learning. This, in turn, will help mitigate the levels of imperfection that are likely to occur in times of emergencies. By cultivating classroom norms that improve the transportability of education from one location to another, we can create a reliable and predictable foundation to serve as an anchor when students and staff are faced with the enormity of deeply unsettling circumstances, such as community health crises, natural disasters, or in-school violence.

A Continuation of Education Plan will ensure that the stability of school norms will follow students to satellite classrooms and in-home remote schooling; but we need to provide an additional safety net of counseling resources to allow them to process their shared trauma by thinking, speaking, discussing, and sharing their feelings out loud with others. Students' sense of safety will be based, in part, on feeling welcome to truthfully express their impressions of the state of their current circumstances. Developmentally, children and young adults need assistance to make sense of the things that occur in their daily lives under "normal" conditions. How much more support do they need in those times when many are yearning for safety? When circumstances rattle students to their core, is it fair to expect them to be capable of sustaining their focus on their education? If the answer is no, then the solution is that schools and communities must come together to support students and restore their equilibrium—for the benefit of their education and for their individual health.

While the exact plan for providing students with mental health counseling should be developed by child psychologists, developmental specialists, pediatricians, and other experts, some general common-sense guidelines are readily apparent. Though improved mental health support services are needed even during "normal" times, when a crisis occurs it is especially important for students to receive some form of in-class group counseling that explains the current crisis and gives kids of all ages the opportunity to ask questions, express their feelings, and openly talk about the situation.

In the case of COVID, these sessions would have been a good place to educate students about disease-prevention measures (such as wearing masks) and let them openly discuss how they feel about the need to wear masks and use social distancing. Providing time and space to allow students to share what they feel—including their apprehensions and fears—would let them know it is natural to be in a state of discomfort during crises, but that it is also possible to take action to protect one's self and one's community.

In addition to the group counseling sessions, teachers, school staff, and family members should also look for signs that students are experiencing depression, elevated states of anxiety, or other behaviors that warrant one-to-one counseling—and make sure they get it *immediately*. Every school should partner with counseling centers, pediatricians, crisis management intervention specialists, and other experts to develop a counseling intervention plan. Start with a skeletal model, if needed, but get some form of counseling in place at schools immediately. In particular, special care and counseling sessions have to be a priority for students who have lost a family member, friend, or neighbor.

While being away from school for an extended time was a different kind of loss for many students, we must not underestimate the emotional and psychological cost endured by students who were unexpectedly and abruptly untethered from a space with routines and opportunities to socialize with their peers. It was more than a way of life. It was an environment they relied on for predictability and guidance. Attending school five days each week from kindergarten through high school cultivated a sense of being surrounded by and rooted in institutions that established a way of life. Educational experiences may have differed from one student to the next, but the loss of their school in a time of a seriously dangerous health pandemic took away an important institutional anchor. As if contending with COVID was not catastrophic enough, students were forced to experience a health crisis that was totally foreign to them while learning a new education system that was also foreign to them. The resumption of education inside of schools may have brought a sigh of relief to many, but countless numbers of students returned to school still frightened and wearing the scars of wounds we cannot see. But it is the uncertainty about whether or not it will happen again that likely will impede the healing process. Those who appear unfazed are not immune. Their scars are right beneath the surface of a new layer of skin they grew while they were away from school. It's a form of survival, but let's not kid ourselves. That new layer of skin, while intended to hide wounds incurred during school closures, is as fragile as those who returned in obvious pain and full of anguish about their futures.

As COVID has shown, a pandemic alters the landscape of what has been normally expected of institutions. Therefore, for the sake of those visibly wounded and those who grew a new layer of protective skin, schools need to expand their responsibilities to include counseling of all students and providing parents and teachers with resources they can use to comfort students as they navigate their way through a terrain that is still totally foreign to everyone. Providing mental health services in schools is important not just for students' well-being, but because it can help save lives. Sometimes it is necessary to shift our focus from the way we traditionally think of education to a form of educational counseling. It could help to allow students to set aside their role as students in stressful times and engage with them as people looking for help trying to endure a crisis. If they wish to confide in adults at school, we should make time to pause, listen, and show empathy. If teachers and other staff members need suggestions about coping strategies that will safely bring a student who confides in them to the other side of a crisis, the advice of professional development specialists can serve as their safety net. The ability to provide compassionate assistance to others in need of help recovering does not have to be the sole responsibility of one person. Remember, it takes a village to raise a child.

Conclusion

OUR BEST CHANCE OF DISRUPTING THE CYCLE OF CONDEMNING poor students to a lifetime of poverty and unmet potential is to provide every student with equitable access to quality educational resources—everywhere and at all times. The transformative staffing model introduced in this book is an essential link for achieving the exceptional schools and classrooms our students deserve.

The idea of closing academic achievement gaps is not a foreign concept. What's foreign is the *how* of making that process happen. Fearing the tendency to overpromise and underdeliver, I've endeavored to describe a straightforward process for *how* to achieve that goal. As simple as it may sound, the first step in the process of closing achievement gaps starts—for both the specialists and teachers—with the most accessible source of information: samples of student work done daily and in classrooms. In my proposed system for closing achievement gaps, students are granted the freedom to demonstrate what they learned while also revealing areas they did not understand and may need further instruction in. No failure is assigned, because errors are no longer used to determine what grade to assign. Errors are evidence that something more is needed. It could be time, instruction, or a different method of instruction. In some cases, it might be a combination of additional time and instruction.

As with the introduction of anything new in our education system, inevitably impediments will be encountered during the initial phase of change. But change is necessary. Creating additional staffing positions to support the professional development of teachers, staff members, and school leaders is just one area where potential obstacles need to be removed. Cultivating exceptional classrooms and schools will require a range of assistance from federal, state, and local officials, working in tandem with school district leaders, in the form of funding and then getting out of the way to allow changes to proceed.

If we ever intend to truly grapple with how to improve the quality of education in underperforming schools, it will require two radically different approaches. The first is to be committed to examining what *educational efficacy* truly means. That conversation needs to happen in every school district and in colleges and universities responsible for training future educators. The second radically different approach is to make attainment of educational efficacy a standard. Without educational efficacy, it will be impossible to earn the trust of students when we want them to take greater responsibility for their learning.

Instituting efficacy standards would be equivalent to providing students and their families with a promissory note, for which a receipt will be owed to them and collected at the end of a 13-year journey that concludes with a diploma truly earned.

In addition to the educational efficacy standards required of schools and districts, it may be fair to require oaths from students and their families to make an earnest effort to develop rigorous learning habits to improve each student's work ethic. The diploma will serve as a symbol representing an educational oath taken and kept by teachers and parents. The 13-year, labor-intensive educational effort is not the sole responsibility of educators. It also belongs to students and their families. The family-and-teacher partnership plan described in *America's Educational Crossroads* delineates each partner's role and responsibility to actively engage everyone in closing academic achievement gaps.

When everyone becomes an active stakeholder in the belief that our public education system can be reimagined in ways needed to close learning gaps, sustained investment in eradicating those gaps will follow. Closing learning gaps will be a tribute to our dedication and determination to achieve our collective goal to propel our system to reach the highest standards. If we value learning efficacy and make it a foundational concept in our schools, it *will* produce favorable performance outcomes.

We must remain persistent in closing academic achievement gaps in order to ensure that future generations of students view academic success as normal. Normalizing student success is linked to professional development resources that will advance teaching skills and positively impact student performance outcomes. By cultivating exceptional classrooms, we can transform how students experience education. But for their sake, we must start by cultivating an exceptional public education system—and exceptional teachers. To accomplish this, every school should install highly qualified professional development resource specialists to help teachers develop and expand their expertise. Expansion of a teacher's expertise is achievable if the right kind of assistance is provided with the intention of elevating professional skills to the highest level of performance standards. The key is to build a better pipeline of professional development support that is directly linked with resources teachers and other staff members need at the school level.

Appendix:

Roles and Responsibilities of Professional Development Specialists

Overview

THE PURPOSE OF CREATING AND SHARING A *TEMPLATE* OF potential responsibilities, qualifications, competencies, and outcomes for each specialist's role is to make transparent, with as much specificity as is possible, what school staff can and should expect from prospective candidates applying for any professional development specialist position. Transparency can be a way to empower everyone, including those who are qualified and interested in applying for the position, the entire staff, students (at the middle and high school levels), parents and legal guardians, school community partners, and anyone else interested in learning about expectations for each position. Sharing information about what the job entails makes everyone aware of what to hold people accountable for in those positions.

Competency is acquired through experience. Experiences involving any new position will include momentary glitches. When they occur, allow them to be addressed quickly to prevent them from turning into gaps that then become normalized. Errors that are not addressed and then allowed to become normal could potentially create irreparable harm.

Including a detailed description of outcomes intended for each position is less about the job description and more about the quality of work done, which will be demonstrated in the outcome of one's performance. In fact, most job openings describe qualifications required to apply for the position, responsibilities that candidates may need to be experienced in, and a range of other important information about the duties. But little is known in advance about what outcomes are expected and what evaluations will be based upon. Being aware of expectations, in advance, and how they align with performance outcomes is one form of assessing degree of success. Outcomes that are generic or extremely specific are one problem. But outcomes that sound impressive with no basis in what really occurs at the classroom level are based on theoretical expectations, which have little connection to the inner workings of a classroom setting.

Teacher evaluations are performance-based assessments. Specifying responsibilities and outcomes of professional development specialists representing key areas of support, including content, class management, instruction, and addressing achievement gaps, can and should be the main categories targeted for improvement in teacher evaluations. While goals in a teacher's evaluation do not have to be limited to those areas, it makes sense to synchronize each area of service that specialists will provide, by aligning a teacher's goal of improving competency with those areas. It is also why it makes sense to provide transparency, by listing roles, responsibilities, and outcomes, of each specialist position to evaluate the progress of each teacher's performance. There must be some means of determining if specialists are having an impact on a teacher's professional growth toward competency, and at what level.

One criterion related to setting goals for specialist and teacher evaluations is to be sure any potential impediments to the new staffing model are removed. Overall focusing on performance outcomes for specialists and teachers is a way of determining the new staffing model's overall effectiveness. The purpose of specifying outcomes is to help gage whether or not different instructional methods provided by an instructional specialist resulted in improved quality of instruction. If specified outcomes have been achieved, it is evidence of the benefits of exchanging outdated practices with new resources. It also reflects the positive impact of including the new staffing model.

Teacher evaluations should include authentic ways of assessing not only the skills attained but also the degree to which skills are attained. The selection of steps listed in the road map for closing academic achievement gaps described in my first book, *America's Educational Crossroads*, provides a template for improving the quality of education. The outcomes referenced in each of the new positions proposed in the appendix of this book outline benchmarks teachers can strive to attain. Helping teachers achieve professional competency in the key areas represented by specialists will be benefited by a process to monitor each teacher's and staff member's professional growth.

If we want to take the guesswork out of skills targeted for development and determining level of progression towards obtaining "highly qualified" status for standards, specialists and staff members should collaboratively develop rubrics with clearly stated skills needed to acquire high performance levels. Rubrics aligned with standards that reflect the true conditions at the school level are far more pragmatic and realistic for furthering each teacher's and staff member's professional growth. Including targeted benchmarks to gauge level of progression and eventual attainment of targeted skills allows for transparency.

And since we are discussing the topic of evaluations, imagine how less intimidating that process would be if evaluations could be framed as *aspirational road maps*. It can be highly motivational for teachers to perceive evaluations as *aspirational road maps* intended to guide educators along their professional learning curve to be the very best in a career they chose.

The cycles of growth will not be without challenges, but valuing professional growth and appreciation of gains made will incentivize educators to remain in the profession. The ultimate goal of utilizing the services of professional development specialists is the same as the criteria embedded in the aspirational evaluation process: expectation of improved professional skills evident in student performance outcomes.

Content Specialist

Purpose

- The addition of content specialists for each subject—math, science, humanities, history, financial literacy, and technology—is essential for advancing each teacher's depth and breadth of knowledge about subjects he/she is assigned to teach. One of the goals is for the specialist to support a teacher's ability to demonstrate mastery of subjects they teach and successfully transfer their mastery to students. Evidence that students have mastered understanding of content can be assessed in their ability to achieve at high academic standards. The content specialist becomes the conduit between teachers and helping them access and evolve their library of resources to enhance their knowledge, which then is embedded in lessons that enrich the quality education provided to students.

Responsibilities

- Help teachers expand their knowledge of assigned content areas.
- Design assessments.
- Work collaboratively with teachers to design rubrics, or other methods of assessment, to measure their rate of improved proficiency in understanding content.

- Strengthen and expand teachers' knowledge of content across diverse educational platforms.
- Keep highly informed about district standards, including distilling what they mean and ways to align standards with learning objectives in lessons.
- Engage teachers in training sessions focused on linking knowledge of content with standards, targeted skills for development, and performance benchmarks, by grade level.
- Maintain catalogs of current and innovative advances related to content area.
- Assist teachers in selecting and integrating contemporary content with lesson plans.

Qualifications

- Demonstrate a depth of knowledge about the content, standards, and skills targeted for development by grade level.
- Create and share inventory of authenticated traditional and contemporary resources.
- Produce content catalogs; include sources for all resources.
- Support a teacher's ability to demonstrate mastery of subjects they teach. Identify methods of successful transference of teacher's mastery to students. It is highly recommended to embed standards-based rubrics within targeted skills to assess students' skill level achieved for each standard.
- Develop transparent protocols for professional development sessions that specialist will use with teachers to examine, distill, and allow for feedback.
- Invite feedback using a variety of platforms, including digital communication or in-person.
- Be available to research, catalog, and inform teachers about relevant findings related to specific topics planned for instruction.

Outcomes

- Teachers responsible for educating students in any content or subject demonstrate expansion of their knowledge by performing at improved and more proficient rates of instruction of the content.
- Catalogs of current and innovative advances in each content area broaden selection of resources and add to the expertise of teacher knowledge.
- Collaborations among teachers are strengthened through sharing discoveries related to subjects in which each took the initiative to research and explore ways to include new information in lessons.
- Academic-performance, competency-based rubrics identifying standards, skills targeted for development, and process of assessing performance outcomes are uniformly used when presenting samples of student work for the purpose of everyone's developing universal and common understanding of interpreting student performance outcomes.
- Content specialists strengthen and expand teachers' knowledge of the content available across diverse educational platforms.
- Teachers demonstrate their ability to successfully provide accessibility to content using diverse non-digital and digital instructional models. Teachers participate in a three-way collaboration with content and technology specialists to achieve the following:
    - Help teachers gain proficiency in utilizing technology-based education resources, including online, live-streaming platforms and instructional models accessible on the internet.
    - Expand and diversify instruction tailored to the needs of a broad range of student learners.
    - Increase accessibility of content through various electronic and other technology devices.
- Teachers review samples of student work to assess evidence of learning objectives in lesson plan achieved in accordance with performance standards.

Instructional Support Specialist

Purpose

- Instructional support specialists are essential for ensuring the quality of educational resources, instructional methods, and delivery of instruction in all classrooms, including subjects referred to as *specials*—art, gym, and music classes. The primary objective of instructional support specialists is to identify best teaching practices. A major priority is to train new teachers in need of developing teaching skills. Another priority is to build veteran teachers' awareness of contemporary best practices and support diversification of instructional methods to ensure inclusion of all students.

Responsibilities

- Assist teachers in the professional development of instructional skills by providing instructional guidance and templates to use as teaching models.
- Research best instructional practices with proven qualitatively and quantifiably measurable results.
- Identify instructional practices designed to benefit students with complex learning profiles.
- Attend to new teachers' professional growth with developing lesson plans and teaching practices.

- Observe instruction and provide strategies to bolster every student's level of engagement in learning.
- Co-lead weekly meetings with the content specialist to develop instructional practices among same-grade level teachers assigned to teach the same content.
- Raise teachers' performance levels in planning lessons and in identifying diverse educational materials and platforms designed to be inclusive of student learning styles and profiles.
- Identify various instructional methods to enhance and sustain student engagement in learning.
- Show teachers how to scaffold-in elevated levels of rigorous tasks to advance critical thinking skills.
- Prepare lesson templates showing examples of how to organize lessons. Include key elements such as learning objectives, rigorous and intellectually challenging brain-teaser assignments that inspire student curiosity and imagination.
- Make brain-teaser assignments accessible to all students. Demonstrate methods of making all assignments, including brain teasers, accessible to students of all learning levels. Prepare cards listing helpful hints that students of various levels of ability can use to guide them through the steps and enable them to achieve success. Help teachers understand the importance of not excluding any student from partaking in educational activities, by avoiding designating activities, such as brain teasers, for accelerated learners only.
- Expand teachers' awareness of options of student participation in learning models; students need to learn how to work in small learning collaboratives and independently.
- Devote time for students to summarize lessons and provide feedback.
- Review lesson plans to ensure elements previously listed are included on a regular basis.
- Establish professional mentoring networks to build collegiality among new and veteran teachers. Prepare ways to utilize sessions constructively.
- Solicit goals that network members would like their collaborative teams to achieve.
- Guide network members toward learning how to nurture and advance one another along their respective professional learning curves.

Qualifications

- Possess an exemplary teaching background and an expansive understanding of the best practices emanating from traditional, innovative, and contemporary instructional techniques.
- Demonstrate great skill in identifying effective models of instruction for classrooms populated by students with diverse learning profiles.

Outcomes

- All teachers, paraprofessionals, and teaching assistants develop instructional proficiency at levels necessary to ensure that students assigned to them are learning and able to achieve at high academic standards.
- All teachers and supportive staff members responsible for teaching students become proficient instructors.
- Teachers demonstrate progression in competency for planning lessons that include diverse methods of instruction.
- Teachers improve their delivery of instruction, strategies for monitoring student performance, and ability to identify and respond to learning gaps.

Classroom Management Specialist

Purpose

- The classroom management specialist plays a key role in training teachers in the skills required to maintain a positive classroom environment. The ability to socially coexist in a classroom environment that cultivates a sense of safety and trust amongst a group of students is vital to nurturing their healthy maturation and individual self-esteem. Achieving these core essentials of emotional health and well-being in a classroom setting relies on teacher guidance and student understanding about social norms that usually require the ability to live within a set of norms that make clear the existence of boundaries which are provided within routines.

Responsibilities

- Work with teachers to cultivate socially responsive and responsible students capable of working independently and collaboratively.
- Support teachers in seeking recommendations from students regarding contributions they can make to create and maintain a safe and welcoming environment for all students.
- Help teachers set expectations, including how to convey safe and welcoming messages, and develop achievable routines to support all students in an opportunity to have a positive educational experience.

Appendix: Classroom Management Specialist

- Routinely observe classrooms.
- Train teachers in classroom-management strategies. Provide follow-up and ongoing consultation to new teachers who are novices in classroom-management skills. If acceleration of classroom-management-skills development is warranted, make it a priority.
- Support teachers' advancement of observation and listening skills.
- Focus on improving teachers' ability to proactively look for signs of potential problems at the earliest stage and initiate steps to prevent disruptions to learning.
- Conduct weekly training sessions to address inappropriate behavioral incidents. Welcome requests to meet daily to advise new teachers and staff members about strategies to defuse and better manage current behavioral issues. Behavior issues don't occur in convenient weekly cycles enabling delays of urgently needed interventions.
- Equip teachers with strategies for de-escalating problems and preventing them from going from bad to worse, while concurrently bolstering their confidence of being in control.
- Teach communication strategies that allow teachers to take command of situations without personalizing a student's behavior.
- Train all staff members in de-escalation techniques through calm and respectful communication skills.
- Convey to teachers their need to remain calm and poised as a technique for reassuring everyone's sense of safety. Be explicit with teachers about the need, and benefit, of having the matter start and remain within the control of adults present.
- Share a broad range of effective management techniques teachers can use that result in allowing all persons involved to retain their dignity. When a teacher/staff member remains in control of a situation, using respectful intervention strategies, they earn the respect of students involved in or witnessing the situation. Acts of humanity, witnessed by students, makes those acts and the person who uses them more memorable.
- With the help of instructional support specialists, impress upon teachers, and particularly new teachers, the valuable impact of normalizing class routines to establish stability.
- Help teachers establish and communicate routines and expectations, which are important because they bring structure, instructionally and behaviorally, to the day-to-day operations of classroom management. Routines also make expectations

predictable for all students, regarding what to expect and when it should be expected. In fact, for most students, the absence of clear expectations and routines can lead to uncertainty, which in turn forces them to try to interpret what they think or guess is expected of them, without the benefit of some form of guidance.

- Orient all staff members about the possibility of academic-related disruptive behaviors. Instructing adults to refrain from overly casting broad aspersions can be achieved by first assessing behavioral conduct in each class. When students show a pattern of experiencing behavioral issues in some classes but not in those where they are experiencing academic success, it is a possible indicator of behavior being related to academic frustration.

- Acquaint teachers with ways to approach problems if there is evidence of academic frustration. In some instances, it may be useful to include content specialists and instructional specialists to advise teachers about detecting whether or not there is a corresponding link between academic underperformance and escalation of inappropriate behaviors. In classes where there is evidence of the student's experiencing academic challenges, consider an academic intervention plan as the initial step needed to address the student's academic frustration.

Qualifications

- Skilled in assisting teachers with assessing students' learning and behavioral profiles.

- Able to conduct trainings to equip all staff members with skills to discern if learning frustrations are potentially linked to behavioral disruptions.

- Capable of specifying indicators that may trigger the emergence of behavior disruptions. Whenever a behavioral incident occurs, can identify a fair process that includes inquiries into what preceded the incidents: Was there provocation by others? Does the student have a predisposed tendency to respond angrily to any slight, whether minor or major? Do anger management issues, and/or a pattern of disruptive behaviors, occur during certain classes?

- Capable of preparing teachers and staff members to be responsive to a range of potential findings. Whether or not there is a direct causality that can be attributed to academic challenges, the unifying perception of all adults is, "the problem is fixable."

- Expertise must include helping teachers become cognizant of initially responding to any incident by searching for the root cause. Any disciplinary process that immediately goes directly to consequences without determining the root cause is likely to punish the student for something; but ultimately, did the response ever have a chance to address and truly change the thing that mattered most? If not, expect a recurrence of incidents that never received the correct remedy to allow the full healing of the wounds resulting from one incident to another. The cycle can be stopped by taking the time to thoroughly investigate root causes. Research and review successful conflict resolution models that focus on unveiling root causes. See 9-R's Conflict Resolution Model, available on the author's website, ImagineAMorePromisingFuture.com.
- Able to identify the *what* that has occurred and the reasons why, before applying a remedy.
- Effective in sharing prevention and intervention strategies, prior to incidents, and in role-play to assess degree of comfort with deploying strategies.
- Build and strengthen every teacher's degree of comfort with intervention strategies. The safety of all students is the priority. Strategies for clearing classrooms during incidents where students are exhibiting unsafe behaviors are useful when direct intervention puts teacher's personal safety at risk. Able to devise strategies for clearing classrooms during incidents where students are exhibiting unsafe behaviors, in order to avoid risking the personal safety of the rest of the students, as well as the teacher.
- Share ways to identify students needing immediate attention and consult with teacher, as needed, about the type of strategies to apply. Whether disruptive behaviors occur at the start of the school year or students uncharacteristically appear on their teacher's radar indicating their need for increased attention later, have everyone fully trained and prepared to use intervention techniques.

Outcomes

- Students become acclimated to routines and are able to predict how the day will unfold.
- Policies serve as effective guardrails delineating boundaries about what is acceptable and unacceptable behavior.

- Routines, schedules, and policies successfully contribute to the stabilization of classroom norms and reflect the quality of social interactions between teacher and students and students with their peers.
- Teachers and staff members clearly understand that cultural norms do not materialize out of thin air but instead typically start with clearly enunciated expectations and classroom policies.
- Teachers have successfully established positive and healthy cultural norms in their classroom by focusing on character building. Classroom pledges listing behaviors all students are encouraged to abide by, to contribute to a class that is safe and welcoming, are evident in everyone's conduct.
- Seeing and saying the behaviors listed in a class pledge have clearly transitioned from words to actions.
- Teachers solicit suggestions from students about positive contributions they can take responsibility for, to ensure the overall well-being of the class where everyone feels welcome and safe. When students contribute their suggestions, they are often more willing to own and accept responsibility.
- Teachers actively support each student's commitment to uphold mutually agreed-upon acts of positive contributions by utilizing social interactions in lessons to strengthen students' reliance on one another: expressing encouragement, respectfully agreeing to disagree when they have different perspectives, listening without interrupting others, and working collaboratively.
- Students understand how being inclusive of their peers' right to their own opinions and ideas is a sign of maturity and respect.
- Students have deepened appreciation of being on the receiving end of considerate and respectful actions from their peers, which adds value to everyone's educational experience.

Inclusion Support Specialist

Purpose

- Whether students differ in size, hair color, height, learning preferences, ethnicity, religion, mobility, learning profiles, musical taste, or in so many other ways we have come to accept one another, opening minds tends to open new doors for them. The inclusion support specialist, prone to be sensitive towards people experiencing a sense of constantly being viewed as "other," is a valued source for students and staff who need to learn how to welcome, embrace, and normalize the presence of every person's unique individuality.

Responsibilities

- Provide overview of Individual Education Plans (IEPs).
- Clarify every area in need of support.
- Ensure that resources are readily available and operating at full capacity.
- Orient all teachers (including art, music, and physical education), ancillary support staff, cafeteria staff, and other staff about the extraordinary attributes that are evident or not visibly evident in each special-needs student's character.
- Specify types of resources that would accompany special-needs students everywhere in school.

- Ensure that practice sessions are made available for teachers and staff members to learn how to operate resources.
- Include in meetings appropriate-age students (middle and high school), parents, or designated family members responsible for the well-being of their child, teen, son, or daughter.
- Create IEPs that will build co-ownership and full investment from all participants.
- Coordinate biweekly meetings with teachers and instructional support specialist, content specialists, technology specialist, classroom management specialist, academic achievement specialist, and principal to assess the student's academic progress, complications that arise, and a plan for addressing complications. Specifically identify who is responsible for supervising each task and reporting outcomes, as some form of systemic monitoring tends to motivate those who are assigned tasks to elevate their level of participation.
- Identify additional resources needed to address unanticipated barriers, which are likely to occur.
- Consult with teachers about social integration of the special-needs students.

Qualifications

- Trained and certified in special education; experienced veteran special-education teachers are particularly recommended because of their years of experience.
- Experienced in consulting with teachers and other staff members about the range of support needed to accommodate those with physical, mental, social, and emotional challenges and ways they affect academic challenges.
- Assertive in addressing discriminatory words, actions, and other misguided perceptions by people who denigrate other people for any reason; and explicit about the various limitations imposed on those who are disabled and how attitudes impair a special-needs student's ability to coexist with others and impede their ability to learn when conditions do not allow them to feel safe and welcome.
- Skilled in the ability to transform opinions. Stereotypical barriers include people who mask concern by appearing sympathetic but do not understand their need to stop viewing the plight of

others through a lens of sympathy, and not talk of how much the student is admired for how well they cope with the obstacles their condition demands of them. So many people need help shifting their view to a new perspective that better serves the true interests of those for whom they claim to feel sorry. In fact, expressions of sympathy do not result in unlocking disabled people from the restrictive constraints imposed on them by sympathizers who then do nothing to remove barriers that prevent them from showing their true abilities. Utterances of "Oh you poor thing" devalue the real wealth of potential possessed by others when they are seen through a lens that doesn't allow for a more panoramic view.

- Changing minds will lead to changing habits. Able to help school build new habits that will lead to successful integration of all students, representative of every citizen across all populations.
- Capable of gauging adults' level of sensitivity.
- Skilled in changing staff and student perceptions about the disabled being able, when in fact obstacles impact their ability to access learning, such as the inability to travel safely throughout the school, or other impediments that obstruct their ability to independently navigate to and from spaces.
- Prepared to provide guidance to staff, regarding how to listen and watch for subtle or discreet comments and behaviors that target disabled or other students.
- Social icebreaking done in the initial stages of a welcome plan will potentially reduce the number of interventions needed to address future acts of intentionally unkind behaviors among students.
- Prepared to teach adults the important prevention strategy of recognizing a need for preplanned guardrails to steer students from statements or behaviors that could be offensive and hurtful.

Outcomes

- Regular classroom visitations that normalize the presence of the inclusion support specialist, who can become familiar with the entire student population. Familiarity of students and their personalities can be useful in helping teachers not only identify students who could potentially misstep over socially inappropriate boundaries but also plan ways to prevent potentially emotional and hazardous situations from occurring.

- Inclusion specialists' class visits will include assigning specialists to work with groups of students. If such specialists are included in lessons, it is suggested they be allowed to alternate being assigned to clusters of students with and without special education students; special education students do not wish to feel as though the extra adult is specifically assigned to monitor them.

- All students want opportunities to just blend in with the normal routines of the day. For an adult to be in tow on a full-time basis would completely cramp the special-needs student's style and could cause the student to be labeled or stigmatized by peers. So please don't do that; it's counterintuitive to the mission of everyone's adapting to a diverse landscape that will eventually lead to the normalization of being among others who share similarities while being different in other ways.

- Visitors to schools where the inclusion support specialist has made inclusion of all students and staff a priority will notice the culture of mutual respect afforded to everyone, regardless of differences, while still seeing differences through a lens of respect. It isn't as if differences are not present or noticed. They are present, and then all parties learned how to get along and peacefully coexist and were rewarded by the positive impact it had on the school's truly welcoming and safe culture.

Academic Achievement Specialist

Purpose

- Academic achievement specialists are the positions needed to make closing academic achievement gaps a reality. The way we succeed in educating all students is to assign an expert who can make sense of and transform data to reveal academic areas in need of strengthening into a remedial plan capable of changing the trajectory of performance profiles, transforming students who are currently languishing in failure, into potentially highly educated scholars. The ability to set the performance bar high, for students and teachers, needs the support of an educational process designed to create pathways for students to achieve standards at the highest level. In addition to having a plan, schools need academic achievement specialists dedicated to monitoring every student's educational progression on a regular basis and responding to lapses that signal a student is in danger of being left behind. Closing academic achievement gaps should have always been and must always be the highest priority of every educational institution.

Responsibilities

- Oversees and manages advancing the school's Academic Achievement Plan.
- Leads teacher collaborative meetings.

- Assists the collaborative in establishing academic, competency, and performance standards.
- Establishes standards-based academic, competency, and performance rubrics.
- Gathers and shares academic achievement performance data for students falling behind.
- Ensures the learning progress of all students schoolwide.
- Assesses what and how well students are learning in schools.
- Consults with teachers about strategies for effective remediation.
- Identifies multiple forms of assessments (competency, academic, and other types of performance-based standards) that will capture a broader and more accurate portrait of what students are capable of achieving.
- Provides standards-based rubrics that include measurable outcomes to ensure improved academic performance.
- Conducts professional development trainings to support the creation of learning cultures.
- Teaches teachers how to teach good study habits to students.
- Conducts and oversees remediation.
- Helps students self-assess their learning experience, including strengths and areas in need of improvement.
- Identifies and implements adaptive technology to support access to content in classes.
- Endeavors to take into consideration and propose a plan of non-academic support, such as counseling, for circumstances students experience that impact their academic performance.
- Teaches all staff members to recognize the connection other circumstances may have on hindering learning or the ability to focus, particularly during testing.
- Preceding remediation plans, addresses the root causes of social or emotional problems, which, if unaddressed, will continue to impede a student's ability to progress along their learning curve.

Appendix: Academic Achievement Specialist

Qualifications

- Ability to monitor intervention policies and practices to improve academic performances of the school's entire student population.
- Experienced in a variety of data analysis, recordkeeping, and other pertinent skills for examination and accurate interpretation of performance outcomes on a range of assessments, including student work products for classes, class tests, and state-mandated standardized assessments.
- Skilled in preparing reports, clearly explaining and acclimating all staff members to the Academic Achievement Plan to ensure full understanding of every element of standardized assessment reports.
- Ability to familiarize every staff member with components of the plan; protocols for deciphering information; the purpose of clustering populations into aggregates and disaggregates by grade level, gender, race, and/or ethnicity; whether they receive free or reduced-cost lunch; and other information.
- Functioning as an essential resource for guiding school policies that include standards for what qualifies as mastery or degree of high competency attained, how to capture and quantify data assessing performance levels, detecting evidence of what students demonstrate they know and how well they know it, and whether or not it meets the designated standard of mastery or high competency.

Outcomes

- Schoolwide policies that identify steps to detect and analyze learning gaps, are fully understood by all teachers and support staff. Instructional remedial plans are aligned with and tailored to performance monitoring systems designed to accurately track student progress.
- Time is devoted to discussing, with a team of teachers and other specialists, extenuating circumstances for students whose test performance might have been impacted by personal or other issues that may have interfered with their ability to focus while taking a test or completing class assignments.

- Preparation of Aspirational Benchmark Achievement Plan for students and their families. The purpose of the Aspirational Benchmark Achievement Plan, which represents similar elements to those in the Academic Achievement Plan, is intended to be a student-friendly version, developed to elevate enthusiasm and motivation to meet goals within specified timelines. Engaging students and families in tracking benchmark results will increase investment in learning.
- Performance tracking systems that provide visible, tangible, and targeted (or aspirational) goals for teachers, students, and family members to work collaboratively to achieve.
- All stakeholders are unified around a plan that enunciates the task of what each team member of the collaborative can do to contribute to the student's learning progression, while also monitoring the actual progress made.
- Student performance is assessed to determine the degree of gains made toward achieving successful academic progress.
- The academic achievement specialist works with each teacher to ensure sustainable mastery levels for the students, as well as the ability to demonstrate that the students have successfully overcome any learning gaps.
- Advocating for the creation of Schoolwide Achievement Plan explained in simple terms for all students and families. Explicitly state what standards mean, their purpose, how student performances are assessed in accordance with standards, and how students can achieve qualitative outcomes by monitoring their performance in their Aspirational Benchmark Achievement Plan.
- Standards are translated into student-friendly and accessible language in accordance with each grade level. Infographic models of each Achievement Plan Template are built with teachers. The Achievement Plan Templates are unveiled at a school assembly the first week of school and help orient students and families about the goals of each plan, to achieve the highest standards.
- The Aspirational Benchmark Achievement Plan is introduced to launch partnerships with school staff, students, and families. The achievement plans become one of the special hallmarks of the school. Convey how all plans have the same goal to improve academic performance outcomes for all students throughout the school year. Designate a special display area for friends, families, and visitors of the school to view each version of the achievement plan. Build their expectations for successful outcomes by allowing them to appreciate what the entire school population intends

to achieve. Request a promise from visitors to contribute their support in helping the entire student population achieve their high academic aspirations. When schools and their communities are united around the same purpose, encouraging and celebrating success, they exemplify the ways "It can take a village to raise a child."

Acknowledgments

THE SLAP HEARD AROUND THE WORLD WAS NOT WHAT OCCURRED at the Oscars. It was the one I received from one of my editors, who, after sending back my manuscript for revisions, figuratively slapped me and said, "Now leave it alone!" See, I had a habit of adding new portions to my manuscript I thought were worthy of mentioning.

My wonderful journey continued while writing *Cultivating Exceptional Classrooms*, my second of three educational books. The acknowledgments included in my first book, *America's Educational Crossroads*, overflowed with such immense appreciation for the support of the talented people in the independent publishing network who ushered me through one of the most unexpected and extraordinary journeys as a newbie to the writing profession. And it was so worthwhile! That was my freshman year. My sophomore year was a bit more harrowing, due mostly to a few self-inflicted wounds brought on by a few instinctively unwise choices I had made. Fortunately, I found a way to attend to my wounds by offering a sincere apology.

Cultivating Exceptional Classrooms contains a broad range of topics, but all are interconnected with the inequities of a public education system rooted in unfair biases. Organizing all of the content was labor-intensive, making the entire editing process an enormous challenge. But what I found especially gratifying is the quality of work each editor did on my behalf, making it evident that they believe in my mission. That is what matters most to me as an author. And it is why I choose to credit everyone who worked with me to elevate my writing while maintaining the essence of my message and respecting my narrative style as a writer. My writing style is not tethered to many of the writing norms, and that makes the editing and other tasks complicated. Fortunately, those I've had the good fortune to work with recognized my tendency to toil through what may be an unorthodox writing process. It is to my editors and creative book designer I owe such high praise. Their contributions went well beyond the service they were hired to provide. While I still have much to learn, the guidance and advice they gave was always appreciated and beyond my expectations.

Lastly, I would like to thank you, my readers, for deciding to read this book, whether out of curiosity or true interest in the missing links I unmask to improve the quality of education. Hopefully, I have succeeded in capturing your attention and inspiring you to engage in discussions about steps to improve our education system. We need our collective wisdom to reimagine a public-school education system that values equity and educational prosperity for all of America's children.

About the Author

JULIE COLES is currently an independent publisher and author of educational books. After retiring from the teaching profession where she held positions as a special education teacher, classroom consultant, vice principal, and headmaster, she made a seamless transition to becoming a writer. Having a fondness for thinking of and implementing innovative ideas to improve the quality of education, Julie was afforded time in retirement to write about new ideas for rebuilding America's public education system.

As Julie progressed along her professional educational journey, many of her innovative ideas were well received. Her professional development presentations for leaders and teachers at district conferences attracted large audiences and requests for follow-up visits to schools. Providing educational consulting services to K–12 teachers and school principals led to opportunities to work collaboratively with staff to strengthen teaching strategies to engage all students in learning. The staff were able to discover the correlation between students fully engaged in learning and the positive impact it had on their classroom's culture.

In addition to the positive responses received for the successful outcomes of her innovative ideas and strategies shared in schools, Julie also earned special recognition from various distinguished organizations.

Some of her many honors and awards include induction into the University of Connecticut Chapter–Phi Delta Kappa; Massachusetts Teacher of the Year (MTY) Runner Up, and the City of Cambridge Mayor's Citation in recognition of that distinction; Edward Calesa Foundation Terrific Teachers Award; and Boston Private Industries Council (PIC) Award. Julie was featured in the article, "Gains are Measurable in This Special Education Setting," published in the Teaching Tools–Learning section of the *Boston Globe Sunday Magazine*; and she served as a panelist on the *Boston Foundation Educators and Community Resources Televised Forum* for NECN TV. She was the keynote speaker for Harvard University Principals' Center, and she delivered the keynote address at her high school's convocation.

One of her most treasured honors was receiving special praise from Boston Public Schools' Superintendent, Dr. Carol Johnson, who shared with one of Julie's recent graduate students, "Ms. Coles is a special school leader because she inspires others to aspire."

Julie's first published book, *America's Educational Crossroads*, introduces readers to the possibility of improving our public education system by linking the reservoir of exceptional educational resources of our current century to many public schools tethered to an era of outdated policies. We can no longer stand by and allow the continuation of widening academic achievement gaps that constrain students' ability to move forward and select from a broad menu of college and career options that can free them from a life of poverty. Quality education that opens access to future employment opportunities can be instrumental in removing decades-old barriers. But *access* to quality education requires shifting our focus to a new way of educating all students residing in every zip code across our country, and this book offers a promising path.

Cultivating Exceptional Classrooms: Unmasking Missing Links to Achieve Quality Education is Julie's second published book. It addresses the impact of teachers' leaving schools, and particularly the disruption in education for untold numbers of students. In an effort to reverse the trend of teacher departures and bolster enrollment in teacher education programs at the college level, Julie proposes far-reaching changes in how districts provide professional development support to school staff.

A future book planned for publication is *Changing Misconceptions About the Principal's Office: A Lifeline for Teachers When the Cavalry of Support Doesn't Arrive*.

For more information about the author, visit
ImagineAMorePromisingFuture.com

www.ingramcontent.com/pod-product-compliance
Lightning Source LLC
Chambersburg PA
CBHW050243010526
44107CB00032B/1390/J